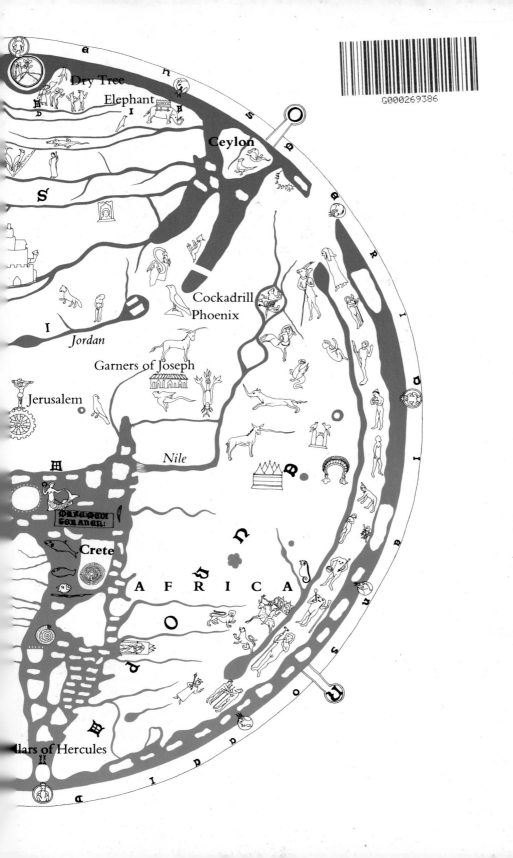

Dry Tree

Elephant

Ceylon

S

I

Jordan

Cockadrill

Phoenix

Garners of Joseph

Jerusalem

Nile

Crete

A F R I C A

O

Pillars of Hercules

THE TRAVELS OF SIR JOHN MANDEVILLE

Introductory picture to the Livre des Merveilles. The illustration shows a traveller, who may have been Mandeville, setting forth.

THE TRAVELS OF
Sir John Mandeville

AN ABRIDGED VERSION WITH COMMENTARY

BY

NORMAN DENNY

AND

JOSEPHINE FILMER-SANKEY

Collins

ST JAMES'S PLACE, LONDON

William Collins Sons & Co Ltd
London · Glasgow · Sydney · Auckland
Toronto · Johannesburg

ISBN 0 00 192329 3

Made and printed in Great Britain by
William Collins Sons & Co Ltd Glasgow

CONTENTS

ILLUSTRATIONS

All the illustrations in this book have been taken from the Livre des Merveilles, which is an illustrated collection of stories of fourteenth-century travellers including Mandeville and several of his sources, among them Marco Polo and Odoric. The collection appears to have been made under the patronage of the Duke of Burgundy somewhere towards the end of the fourteenth century, and is now in the Bibliothèque Nationale in Paris.

INTRODUCTION

IT IS ON RECORD that when Leonardo da Vinci moved from Florence to Milan in 1499 one of the forty books he took with him was *The Travels of Sir John Mandeville*. The book was then well over a hundred years old, having been written in the 1360s. French, Latin, English and probably German and Italian manuscript versions had long been in circulation, and with the introduction of printing it may be said to have entered the class of 'world best-sellers'; indeed, it was probably the first European book to do so. It continued to be widely read for some centuries. Shakespeare and Bunyan are two of the many English writers who in one way or another made use of it. Its influence on western literature has been pervasive and profound.

Today it is still a living book, not merely a source-book for specialists, but one that can be read with pleasure by readers of any kind and almost any age. But its status has altered. We no longer think of it, as men did for centuries, as a book of travel or a work of geography or history. Its value lies in the quality of the writing and the picture it evokes of the mind and colour, the beliefs, myths and legends, the whole imaginative climate of the Christian world in the Middle Ages.

But it is a work enclosed in mystery. Who wrote it? In what language was it originally written? How much travelling, if any, did the author really do?

The first two questions, fascinating though they are, are not of the first importance. The book itself is what matters, the magnificent book and the character of the author that emerges so sturdily from its pages. We should be little the wiser for knowing his true name and address, his nationality (in an age when the word had no meaning) and the circumstances of his private life.

But the questions cannot be dismissed. The problem of authorship cannot be ignored, if only because anyone consulting an encyclopedia or other standard work of reference is likely to come upon something like this: '*The Travels of Sir John Mandeville*, a spurious book of travel generally attributed to Jean (or Jehan) de Bourgogne, a Belgian physician living and practising in Liège, who was also known as "John of the Beard".'

The inference is that we are dealing with two separate men; and the reasons which have caused many reputable scholars to incline to the view that the author of the book was not an English knight from St Albans, but a different person altogether, are intricate but certainly not conclusive. They are based on discrepancies and contradictions between the earliest manuscript versions, in French, Latin and English; on clues and half-hints contained in one version or another; on family trees and church inscriptions, and above all on the testimony of a somewhat dubious character called Jean d'Outremeuse, a writer of historical works who claimed that the Belgian, Jean de Bourgogne, told him on his death-bed that he was really Sir John Mandeville, 'Count of Montfort in England, Lord of the Isle of Campdi and of Château Perouse' (titles which, so far as we know, John Mandeville did not possess).

To pursue the argument in detail would take us far beyond the scope of this volume, and in any case the present editors are not convinced by it. There is a simpler possibility.

The first Mandeville known to history, or to English history, was a Norman gentleman who came to England with William the Conqueror in 1066. The family settled in England, multiplied and prospered, acquiring estates in Devon and other parts of the country, notably in the counties adjacent to London. A Mandeville became Earl of Essex. They made influential marriages and they became involved in politics. A certain John Mandeville figures, rather low down, on the list of conspirators pardoned in the year 1312 by King Edward II, following the aristocratic rebellion in which the king's favourite, Piers Gaveston, was murdered. The rebellion was checked but not crushed. Ten years later King Edward met and defeated his enemies, again only temporarily, at the Battle of Boroughbridge, in Yorkshire. Some of the leaders were killed, some were executed and some fled abroad. This was in 1322, the year in which, by his own account, John Mandeville set out on his travels.

He was probably a younger member of the clan, a nephew or cousin of the John Mandeville whose name appeared on that earlier list of conspirators. As a descendant of a Norman family and a member of the English upper class he would have been likely to speak French at least as well as he did English; and being pursued by the king's vengeance he had good reason for adopting another name.

In short, it is entirely possible that Sir John Mandeville and Jean de Bourgogne were one and the same man. The bearded 'Jean de Bourgogne' took refuge in the relative obscurity of Liège, where he studied and practised medicine, achieving some distinction as a doctor, and even, as it seems, writing a medical treatise on the Black Death. When he travelled further (if he did travel further) it was still under his assumed name; and he did not disclose his true identity until his book appeared at the end of his long life.

This is admittedly surmise, but it is a surmise which fits the likely facts. We are dealing with a book, written before the days of printing, which passed through the hands of innumerable copyists, translators and 'editors', some of whom were careless, some ignorant and some inventive on their own account.

The book itself, in no matter which version, tells us virtually nothing about the personal life of the author. On the other hand the different versions contain many contradictions. We learn, for example, from the Prologue to the English version that the author wrote his book originally in Latin, then in French and finally translated it into English, '. . . that every man of my nation may understand it'. The French version tells it otherwise; and it was almost certainly not the case. The first known English version appeared early in the fifteenth century, at least thirty years after the author's death. Moreover, a careful comparison of the texts suggests very strongly that the book was written originally in French and translated into English by another hand.

To escape from the tangle of learned speculation, argument and counter-argument, we have to make up our own minds. This volume will contain no further reference to Jean de Bourgogne. We conclude that the author was John Mandeville, and that he wrote his book in one language only, his own Norman French. Whether he wrote it at his home in St Albans, in Liège or in Rome (all three have been suggested) is not known. Nor is anything known of the learned clerk who turned it into English. Like other translators he has vanished into obscurity; but at least, as a master of the English language, he deserves the tribute of our gratitude and respect.

There remains the important question: did John Mandeville really travel to all the countries which he claims to have visited, and see all the remarkable things he claims to have seen?

Obviously he did not. Many of the things and places he writes about did not exist. The Land of the Amazons, for example, and the Kingdom of Prester John, both of which he describes at some length, were countries of legend, and his vivid account of the latter is based on a forged document.

Truth and fable are inextricably mingled in Mandeville's story. It is likely enough that he went to the Holy Land, and he may also have penetrated into Egypt and Syria. But there is no evidence whatever that he went further – to India, China or the East Indies, to the innumerable islands and teeming cities which he situated in the vast, vague, bewildering regions of 'Ind' and 'Cathay'.

His book, although he pretends otherwise, is not a first-hand book of travel, but a compilation based largely on the works of writers who were genuine travellers. Of these Marco Polo was incomparably the greatest, but there were many others, of whom some account is given in the Appendix. Mandeville, a voracious reader in at least four languages, borrowed from every source that offered, sometimes translating passages almost word for word so that they can be readily identified, but more often re-writing and re-arranging his material, adding details from different sources (or out of his own head) and making the whole into what may be described as a 'romance of travel', a creation of his own, bearing the unmistakable imprint of his mind and personality.

His written sources, the substance of his book, have for the most part been traced; but he must also have picked up a great deal of miscellaneous information by word of mouth, listening to rumour and travellers' tales and perhaps jotting them down for future use. Occasionally he finds it prudent to warn his reader that this was something he did not see with his own eyes, and sometimes he questions, and even disputes, the matter he is reporting. But it does not happen very often. He was always more ready to accept than to reject, and very few tales were too steep for him. He was a shrewd and tolerant but simple-minded man, living in a simple-minded world where almost nothing was too marvellous or terrible, too monstrous or too magical, to be believed.

We have a fantasy picture of that world in the Mappa Mundi, dating from about 1300, of which a drawing is reproduced in this volume. This was Mandeville's world, the world as Christian men saw it and generally preferred to see it, although with Marco Polo and others a wider knowledge was creeping in. Fascinated but also appalled by the immensity of the unknown lying beyond the bounds of Christendom, they clung, with the encouragement of the Church, to the traditional cosmology and their ancient beliefs. But to say that the men of that age were ignorant and credulous is not to say that they were stupid or dull-minded. What they could not see they could imagine. They peopled the unknown world with visions – demons and monsters, saints, miracle-workers and mighty kings, creatures terrifying and utterly strange: and in so doing enriched their own lives. It is not surprising that they were very ready to believe Mandeville, who believed these things himself because they delighted him.

Which brings us to a last question. Is Mandeville to be regarded as a cheat, a liar and a fraud?

All this was eventually said of him, but not for a long time. Even in the seventeenth century Samuel Purchas, an esteemed scholar in his day whose special field was the work of the earliest Christian missionaries, could proclaim him 'the greatest Asian traveller that ever the world had'. But gradually, as knowledge grew, as his sources came to light and his absurdities became manifest, opinion swung to the opposite extreme. Mandeville was laughed at and his book was dismissed as a fabrication, a tissue of lies.

The truth lies between the two extremes.

Sir John Mandeville was a widely-read scholar, a physician, a linguist, a warm-hearted and deeply religious man with a lively interest in the world around him and in all human affairs. In some respects he was far ahead of his time. In an age when Christendom as a whole believed that the earth was flat he sturdily maintained (and demonstrated) that it was round. But above all he was a man of brilliant imagination; a natural writer of such excellence that Dr Johnson, accepting the authenticity of the English version, could call him 'the father of English prose'.

That he borrowed without acknowledgement from the works of other writers is no great matter; it was a common practice in his day. Nor need it be greatly held against him that he based his book on a pretence. He was a writer, and it is as such that he must be judged. He set out to write a book of travel because the subject enthralled him, and he wrote it in the way that suited him best, with himself in the middle of it, seeing with his own eyes and talking with his own voice. He was no more cheating than the novelist who tells a story in the first person. He wanted the story to ring true, because what he wrote was what he believed, or wanted to believe.

It goes without saying that he believed too much, as any man is likely to do whose eyes are intent on splendours beyond the horizon, or monsters lurking in the dark: any man, that is to say, who is by nature a poet. This was the world that he truly explored, not the world of factual history and geography, but the world of mystery and imagination existing in men's minds and in the mind of the times. And he made of it a book so teeming with life and colour and amazement that it has lived for six hundred years.

The original work, in thirty-four chapters, is about eighty thousand words long, and the full text is readily available to the reader who is prepared to work his way through that long course of outmoded English, which tends, in the manner of the time, to be wordy, over-detailed, repetitive and rhetorical. The present version, which includes nearly one third of the original (and, we believe, the best of it) is intended for the reader who shrinks from so much labour but would be glad to know something about Mandeville. The aim has been to convey a faithful impression of the book as a whole, using a linking narrative to bridge the gaps and (briefly) fill in the historical background. Text and commentary are typographically distinguished. The Mandeville text is based on what is known as the 'Cotton' manuscript, dating from the early fifteenth century and now in the British Museum, of which an edited version was produced by Professor A. W. Pollard in 1900. Professor Pollard confined his editing to the modernisation of the spelling and punctuation, and to a very few small alterations, the insertion of a word here and there, where it was obviously called for. Otherwise, as he said, he reproduced the Cotton version 'warts and all'.

The present editors have gone a little further. Where it could be done without injuring the literary style, they have substituted current words for ancient usage – for example, 'called' for 'clept', and 'river' for 'flome'. Where, however, a word or phrase calls for elucidation but cannot be altered without introducing an anachronism, they have left the original intact and added the interpretation in brackets. Apart from this, and although the book has been greatly shortened and its chapter-scheme revised, the excerpts quoted are substantially unchanged; condensations occur only in the commentary, where the major gaps are clearly indicated. Minor omissions, within a paragraph, are sometimes indicated by means of dots. In other cases, where a sentence or two could be simply removed without affecting the continuity or the rhythm of the prose, this has been done.

Our greatest concern, and our greatest problem, has been to preserve without distortion the true quality and essence of Mandeville. His book is a work of poetry as well as of prose, and poetry cannot be tinkered with. What is wonderful is that so little tinkering should have been necessary. Mandeville is far easier to read than his great contemporary, Geoffrey Chaucer. But then, he was an altogether simpler man, and his book was intended not merely for the cultured reader. It was a tale to be read or (more often) listened to by all manner of people, young or old; by anyone and everyone capable of enchantment and delight.

Othello said:

> Wherein of antres vast and deserts idle,
> Rough quarries, rocks, and hills whose heads touch heaven,
> It was my hint to speak . . .
> And of the Cannibals that each other eat,
> The Anthropophagi, and men whose heads
> Do grow beneath their shoulders.

Benedict said, referring unkindly to Beatrice:

'I will go on the slightest errand now to the Antipodes that you can devise to send me on; I will fetch you a toothpicker now from the furthest inch of Asia; bring you the length of Prester John's beard; do you any message to the Pigmies – rather than hold three words conference with this harpy.'

Those passages are a part of the debt that Shakespeare owed to Mandeville; they contain a hint, no more, of the debt we all owe him, we who belong to the western Christian world.

Chapter 1

THE BEGINNING OF THE JOURNEY

Constantinople – The Isles of Greece – The Dragon Maid – The Lands of the Great Soldan – Egypt – The Phoenix – The Pyramids

I, JOHN MANDEVILLE, knight (albeit I be not worthy), that was born in England, in the town of St Albans, and passed the sea in the year of our Lord Jesu Christ, in 1322, in the day of St Michael; and hitherto have been long time over the sea, and have seen and gone through many diverse lands, and many provinces and kingdoms and isles and have passed throughout Turkey, Armenia the little and the great; through Tartary, Persia, Syria, Arabia, Egypt the high and the low; through Amazonia, Ind the less and the more a great part; and throughout many other Isles, that be about Ind; where dwell many diverse folks, and of diverse manners and laws, and of diverse shapes of men. Of which lands and isles I shall speak more plainly hereafter . . . And ye shall understand that I have put this book out of Latin into French, and translated it again out of French into English, that every man of my nation may understand it.

The England John Mandeville left behind him in that year of 1322 was a country torn by dissension, ruled by a weak king at bitter odds with his barons and his scheming, ambitious wife, a king who was destined to be deposed and hideously murdered five years later. It was the century of the Black Death and the Hundred Years' War, but these calamities have no place in Mandeville's book, which was a direct outcome of the stir of wonder and astonishment that was gradually spreading through the West as merchants such as the Polos (first the father and uncle of the great Marco, and then Marco himself), and Christian missionaries such as Odoric and Carpini, brought back accounts of the hitherto unknown East. The bounds of Christian knowledge were being extended, while at the same time a danger was arising in the threat to Christendom represented by Persians, Turks and Saracens in the Near and Middle East, with the Mongols, an unknown quantity, somewhere beyond them. There was much agitation in favour of yet another Crusade to recapture the Holy Places. We find many echoes of this preoccupation in the earlier part of the book, when Mandeville was moving, so to speak, within the compass of the known world. Later, when the story travels deep into the unknown, we hear no more of it.

The first stopping-place, after the reader has been given careful instruction as to the various ways of getting there, is Constantinople, in those days still a Christian stronghold and the capital of the greatly shrunken Byzantine (or Greek) Empire. 'A full fair city,' says Mandeville, 'and a good and well-walled.'

And there dwelleth commonly the Emperor of Greece. And there is the most fair church and the most noble of all the world; and it is of Saint Sophia. And before that church is the image of Justinian the emperor, covered with gold, and he sitteth upon an horse y-crowned. And he was wont to hold a round apple of gold in his hand: but it is fallen out thereof. And men say there, that it is a token that the emperor hath lost a great part of his lands and of his lordships; for he was wont to be Emperor of Roumania and of Greece, of all Asia the less, and of the land of Syria, of the land of Judea in the which is Jerusalem, and of the land of Egypt, of Persia, and of Arabia. But he hath lost all but Greece; and that land he holds only. And men would many times put the apple into the image's hand again, but it will not hold it. This apple betokeneth the lordship that he had over all the world, that is round. And the tother hand he lifteth up against the East, in token to menace the misdoers. This image stands upon a pillar of marble at Constantinople.

At Constantinople is the cross of our Lord Jesu Christ, and his coat without seams, that is called Tunica inconsutilis, and the sponge, and the reed, of which the Jews gave our Lord eysell [vinegar] and gall, on the cross. And there is one of the nails, that Christ was nailed with on the cross.

And some men hold that half the cross, that Christ was done on, be in Cyprus, in an abbey of monks that men call the Hill of the Holy Cross; but it is not so. For that cross that is in Cyprus is the cross on which Dismas the good thief was hanged. But all men know not that; and that is evilly done. For the profit of the offering [i.e. the collecting-box], they say that it is the cross of our Lord Jesu Christ . . .

And one part of the crown of our Lord, wherewith he was crowned, and one of the nails, and the spearhead, and many other relics be in France, in the king's chapel, and the crown lieth in a vessel of crystal richly dight.

The king of France in question was Louis IX, St Louis, and the casket that contained the relics is still in the Sainte Chapelle, the exquisite church he built in the heart of Paris.

The foregoing is only a part of what Mandeville has to tell us about Constantinople; but we may skip his account of the manners and customs of its people. The story moves on by sea through the Aegean amid the isles of Greece, and tells of 'a great hill that men call Olympus', separating Macedonia and Thrace.

Mariners and the adamant

Hunting with leopards. The artist had obviously never seen a leopard and imagined that they resembled dogs.

And it is so high, that it passeth the clouds. And there is another hill, that is called Athos, that is so high that the shadow of him reacheth to Lemne, that is an isle; and it is seventy-six mile away. And at the top of the hill is the air so clear, that men may find no wind [breath] there, and therefore may no beast live there, so is the air dry.

And men say that philosophers sometimes went upon these hills, and held to their nose a sponge moisted with water for to have air; for the air above was so dry. And above in the dust and in the powder of those hills, they wrote letters and figures with their fingers. And at the year's end they came again, and found the same letters and figures, the which they had written the year before, without any default. And therefore it seemeth well that these hills pass the clouds and join to the pure air.

The distance from Mount Athos, where a famous monastery was built, to the island of Lemnos is some sixty miles. Clearly no shadow could have reached so far. But the poetic vision conveys a truth about those historic lands of Greece that no guide-book description could achieve: the purity and stillness of the air in which they are bathed, the calm and limpid clarity. This was Mandeville's order of truth, which illumines all his story.

We come to the first of his great tales, a variant of the tale of Beauty and the Beast, with the sexes reversed.

The Dragon Maid

Some men say that in the isle of Lango is yet the daughter of Ypocras [possibly Hippocrates], in form and likeness of a great dragon, that is a hundred fathom of length, as men say, for I have not seen her. And they of the isles call her Lady of the Land. And she lieth in an old castle, in a cave, and sheweth twice or thrice in the year, and she doth no harm to no man, but if men do her harm. And she was thus changed and transformed, from a fair damosel, into the likeness of a dragon, by a goddess that was called Diana. And men say that she shall so endure in that form of a dragon, unto the time that a knight come that dare to kiss her on the mouth; and then shall she turn again to her own kind, and be a woman again, but after that she shall not live long.

And it is not long since that a knight of Rhodes, that was hardy and doughty in arms, said he would kiss her. And when he was upon his courser, and went to the castle and entered the cave, the dragon lifted up her head against him. And when the knight saw her in that form so hideous and so horrible he fled away. And the dragon bare the knight upon a rock; and from that rock, she cast him into the sea. And so was lost both horse and man.

And also a young man, that knew not of the dragon, went out of a ship, and came to the castle, and came into the cave, and presently he found a chamber; and there he saw a damosel that combed her head and looked in a mirror; and she had much treasure about her. And she turned her toward him and asked him what he would? And he said, he would be her lover. And she asked him, if that he were a knight? And he said, nay. And then she bade him go again unto his fellows, and make him a knight, and come again upon the morrow, and she should come out of the cave before him, and then come kiss her on the mouth and have no dread – for I shall do thee no manner of harm, albeit that thou see me in likeness of a dragon; for though thou see me hideous and horrible to look on, I tell thee that it is made by enchantment; for without doubt, I am none other than thou seest now, a woman, and therefore dread thee nought. And if thou kiss me, thou shalt have all this treasure, and be my lord, and lord also of all this isle.

And he departed from her and went to his fellows to ship, and let make him knight and came again upon the morrow for to kiss this damsel. And when he saw her come out of the cave in form of a dragon, so hideous, and so horrible, he had so great a dread that he fled again to the ship, and she followed him. And when she saw that he did not look back, she began to cry, as a thing that had much sorrow; and then she turned again into her cave. And anon the knight died.

And thenceforward might no knight see her, but that he died anon. But when a knight cometh that is so hardy to kiss her, he shall not die; but he shall turn the damosel into her right form and kindly shape, and he shall be lord of all the countries and isles abovesaid.

The people of Cyprus, who hunted 'with Papynonns, that be like leopards' (and were probably cheetahs) had strange eating habits.

For they make ditches in the earth all about in the hall, deep to the knee, and they do pave them; and when they will eat, they go therein and sit there. And the skill [reason] is that they may be the more fresh; for that land is much more hotter than it is here. And at great feasts, and for strangers, they set forms and tables, as men do in this country, but they had rather sit in the earth.

After this the story and the itinerary become confused. We are in the eastern Mediterranean, in the land of 'Outremer' (beyond the sea) where so many battles had been fought to drive the Moslems out of the Holy Places. For a time Christian principalities like Antioch and Edessa and the kingdom of Jerusalem maintained a foothold in the lands where Christianity was born. But the pressure from the east was too great, and by Mandeville's day the country was entirely in Saracen or Turkish hands, with local rulers and governors owing allegiance to the Turkish Sultan, who did not, however, necessarily forbid Christians to visit it – 'and whoso will go by land through the land of Babylon, where the soldan dwelleth commonly, he must get grace of him and leave to go more siker [safely] through those lands and countries.'

In the account which follows of the soldan, whom we must assume to be the Turkish Sultan, Mandeville introduces one of his rare personal notes, evidently with the idea of establishing his credentials with the reader. He tells us that having fought with distinction in the Sultan's wars he was offered a princess in marriage – an offer which, as a virtuous Christian, he refused. We are given no details, no corroborative evidence of any kind. The fact is that this tale of a high-born unbeliever being offered a Moslem lady in marriage cropped up frequently in medieval romances; also, at the very end of his book, Mandeville confesses to his inadequacy in the arts of war.

His use of the word 'admiral' sounds odd today. Those 'admirals' were emirs or amirs – that is to say, local chieftains and tribal rulers. The title was, as it still is, Amir-al- followed by the name of a place, a tribe or an element. Hence the English word (French 'amiral'). An *Amir-al-bahr* was a chieftain of the sea.

The Soldan

At Babylon there is a fair church of our Lady, where she dwelled seven year, when she fled out of the land of Judea for dread of King Herod. There dwelleth the soldan in a fair castle, strong and great, and well set upon a rock. In that castle dwell alway, to keep it and to serve the soldan, more than 6,000 persons, that take all their necessaries off the soldan's court. I ought right well to know it; for I dwelled with him as soldier in his wars a great while against the Bedouins. And he would have married me full highly to a great prince's daughter, if I would have forsaken my law and my belief; but I thank God I had no will to do it, for nothing that he offered me.

And you must know that the soldan may lead out of Egypt more than 20,000 men of arms, and out of Syria, and out of Turkey and out of other countries that he holds, he may raise more than 50,000. And all those be at his wages, and they be always with him, without the folk of his country, that is without number. And every each of them hath by year the mountance sum of six score florins; but it behoveth that every of them hold three horses and a camel. And by the cities and by towns be admirals, that have the governance of the people; one hath to govern four, and another more, and another well more. And as many [as much money] taketh the admiral by him alone as all the other soldiers have under him; and therefore, when the soldan will advance any worthy knight, he will make him an admiral. And when there is any dearth, the knights be right poor, and then they sell both their horse and their harness.

And the soldan hath four wives, one Christian and three Saracens, of the which one dwelleth at Jerusalem, and another at Damascus, and another at Ascalon; and when they choose they remove to other cities, and when the soldan will he may go to visit them.

And before the soldan cometh no stranger except he be clothed in cloth of gold, or of Tartary or of Camaka [samite], in the Saracens' guise, and as the Saracens use. And it behoveth, that anon at the first sight that men see the soldan, be it in window or in what place else, that men kneel to him and kiss the earth, for that is the manner to do reverence to the soldan of them that speak with him.

But there were greater rulers than this soldan of Babylon and also there was a greater Babylon. Babylon was another name for Cairo, which was situated near the ancient town of Bab-al-yun, founded by the Persian Emperor, Cambyses, in 525 BC. But it also denoted the region of Mesopotamia. Mandeville clears up this confusion in his own fashion, while at the same time, like the showman he was, giving his reader a hint of things to come.

And from Babylon where the soldan dwelleth, to go right between the Orient and the Septentrion [east by north] toward the great Babylon, is forty journeys [days' journey] to pass by desert. But it is not the great Babylon in the land and in the power of the said soldan, but it is in the power and the lordship of Persia, but he holdeth it of the great Chan, that is the greatest emperor and the most sovereign lord of all the parts beyond, and he is lord of the isles of Cathay and of many other isles and of a great part of Ind, and his land marcheth unto Prester John's land, and he holdeth so much land that he knoweth not the end: and he is more mighty and greater lord without comparison than is the soldan: of his royal estate and of his might I shall speak more fully when I shall speak of the land and of the country of Ind.

The story moves on to Egypt, with an admirable account of the seasonal flooding of the Nile Valley, which rendered it so fertile that in the great days of Rome it was known as the granary of the Empire. The belief that the Nile was partly an underground river goes back at least to the time of Alexander.

That river of Nile, all the year, when the sun entereth into the sign of Cancer, it beginneth to wax, and it waxeth always, as long as the sun is in

Cancer and in the sign of the Lion; and it waxeth in such manner that it is sometimes so great that it is twenty cubits or more of deepness, and then it doth great harm to the goods that be upon the land. For then may no man travail to plough the lands for the great moisture, and therefore is there dear [lean] time in that country. And also, when it waxeth little, it is dear time in that country, for default of moisture. And when the sun is in the sign of Virgo, then beginneth the river for to wane and to decrease little and little, so that when the sun is entered into the sign of Libra, then they enter between these rivers. This river cometh, running from Paradise terrestrial, between the deserts of Ind, and after it smiteth unto land and runneth long time many great countries under earth. After it goeth out under an high hill that men call Alothe, that is between Ind and Ethiopia some five months' journey from the entry of Ethiopia; and after it environeth all Ethiopia and Mauritania, and goeth all along from the Land of Egypt unto the city of Alexandria to the end of Egypt, and there it falleth into the sea. About this river be many birds and fowls, as sikonies, that they call ibis.

Egypt is a long country, but it is straight, that is to say narrow, for they may not enlarge it toward the desert for default of water. For it raineth but little in that country, and for that cause they have no water but if it be that of flood of that river. And forasmuch as it raineth not in that country but the air is always pure and clear, therefore in that country be the good astronomers, for they find there no clouds to hinder them.

We learn later what Mandeville has in mind when he talks of 'Paradise terrestrial', the mythical source of the four great rivers which loomed so large in medieval geography. Meanwhile we hear two stories, the first perhaps the most beautiful of all ancient legends.

The Legend of the Phoenix

In Egypt is the city of Heliopolis, that is to say, the city of the Sun. In that city there is a temple, made round after the shape of the Temple of Jerusalem. The priests of that temple have all their writings under the date of the fowl that is called phoenix; and there is none but one in all the world. And he cometh to burn himself upon the altar of that temple at the end of five hundred year; for so long he liveth. And at the five hundred years' end, the priests array their altar honestly, and put thereupon spices and sulphur and other things that will burn lightly; and then the bird phoenix cometh and burneth himself to ashes. And the day next after, men find in the ashes a worm; and the second day next after, men find a bird quick and perfect; and the third day next after, he flieth his way. And so there is no more birds of that kind in all the world, but it alone, and truly that is a great miracle of God. And men may well liken that bird unto God, because that there is no God but one; and also, that our Lord arose from death to life the third day. This bird men see often-time fly in those countries; and he is not mickle more than [not much bigger than] an eagle. And he hath a crest of feathers upon his head more great than the peacock hath; and his neck is yellow after colour of an oriel that is a stone well shining; and his beak is coloured blue as ind [indigo]; and his wings be of purple colour, and his tail is barred across with green and yellow and red. And he is a full fair bird to look upon against the sun, for he shineth full gloriously and nobly.

The Balsam Garden

Also in Egypt be gardens, that have trees and herbs, the which bear fruit seven times in the year. And in that country, and in others also, men find long apples [bananas] to sell in their season, and men call them apples of Paradise; and they be right sweet and of good savour. And though ye cut them in never so many gobbets or parts, overthwart [across] or endlong, evermore ye shall find in the midst the figure of the Holy Cross of our Lord Jesu.

Also besides Cairo, outside that city, is the field where balm groweth; and it cometh out on small trees that be none higher than to a man's breeks' girdle, and they seem as wood that is of the wild vine. And in that field be seven wells that our Lord Jesu Christ made with one of his feet when he went to play with other children. That field is not so well closed but that men may enter as they please; but in that season when the balm is growing men keep guard over it, that no man may enter.

This balm groweth in no place, but only there. And though that men bring of the plants, for to plant in other countries, they grow well and fair; but they bring forth no fruitful thing, and the leaves of balm fall not. And men cut the branches with a sharp flintstone, or with a sharp bone, when men will go to cut them; for whoso cut them with iron, it would destroy their virtue and their nature. And men make always that balm to be tilled by Christian men, or else it would not bear fruit. The Saracens say also, that the balm groweth in Ind the more, in that desert where Alexander spake to the trees of the sun and of the moon, but I have not seen it; for I have not been so far above upward, because that there be too many perilous passages.

The Balsam Garden outside Cairo, which was believed to have been grown from a root given to King Solomon by the Queen of Sheba, was famous in those days, and a source of great wealth to the Sultan. The unique balm was held to possess miraculous qualities. It cured wounds and blindness, mended broken bones and internal injuries, and preserved fresh meat and dead bodies from decay. What follows is in its own way no less remarkable.

The Garners of Joseph

And now also I shall speak of another thing that is beyond Babylon, above the flood of the Nile, toward the desert between Africa and Egypt; that is to say, of the garners of Joseph, that he let make for to keep the grains for the peril of the dear years. And they be made of stone, full well made of masons' craft; of the which two be marvellously great and high, and the other not so great. And every garner hath a gate for to enter within, a little high from the earth; for the land is wasted and fallen since the garners were made. And within they be all full of serpents. And above the garners without be many scriptures [inscriptions] of diverse languages. And some men say that they be sepultures of great lords that were sometime, but that is not true, for all the common rumour and speech, of all the people there, both far and near, is that they be the garners of Joseph; and so find they in their scriptures, and in their chronicles. On the other part, if they were sepultures, they should not be void within, nor should they have gates for to enter within; for ye may well know, that tombs and sepultures be not made of such greatness, nor of such highness; wherefore it is not to believe, that they be tombs or sepultures.

Those garners (or granaries) were in fact the great pyramids of Egypt. Other writers had suggested that they were tombs, but Mandeville would not have it. To his mind it was against all sanity that anyone should have built those enormous structures for no better purpose than to glorify forgotten kings. He stuck to the popular belief based on the Old Testament story of Joseph, who built great barns for the storage of a reserve of grain against the 'dear years' – the lean years, when the Nile valley was either over-flooded or not flooded enough. He was ready to believe so many improbabilities, but in this case, for quite sensible reasons, he refused to accept the truth.

The last thing he has to tell us about Egypt is its alphabet, of which he names the twenty-three letters. Language was a constant preoccupation with Mandeville, but it is one in which we shall not attempt to follow him.

Chapter 2

THE HOLY LAND

The Abbey of St Catherine – The Dry Tree – How Roses came into the World – The Church of the Holy Sepulchre – King Herod – The river Jordan – Nazareth – Moslems and Christians

THE HOLY LAND – Palestine, Syria and Arabia. How far Mandeville's picture of these countries is based on first-hand observation is anyone's guess. What is certain is that he had an ample literature to draw on, and did so extensively, offering his readers a good deal of guide-book information, together with familiar Bible tales. There is a hint of self-consciousness in the writing, as though he were looking over his shoulder, mindful of the fact that he is on well-trodden ground and dare not let imagination or rumour run riot, as he does when, leaving the known world behind, he moves on into the mystery of the deeper East. The chapters that he devotes to the Holy Land contain much that is familiar to any reader of the Old Testament. But there are splendid stories, among them the account of the Abbey of St Catherine, on or near Mount Sinai, which Mandeville tells us was called the Desert of Sin.

The Abbey of St Catherine

Here is the Church of Saint Catherine, in the which be many lamps burning; for they have of oil of olives enough, both for to burn in their lamps and to eat also. And that plenty have they by the miracle of God for the ravens and the crows and the choughs and other fowls of the country assemble them there every year once, and fly thither as in pilgrimage; and each of them bringeth a branch of the bay or of olive in their beaks as an offering, and leave them there; of the which the monks make great plenty of oil. And this is a great marvel.

Also, when the prelate of the abbey is dead, I have understood, by information, that his lamp quencheth. And when they choose another prelate, if he be a good man and worthy to be prelate, his lamp shall light with the grace of God without touching of any man. For each of them hath a lamp by himself, and by their lamps they know well when any of them shall die. For when any shall die, the light beginneth to change and to wax dim; and if he be chosen to be prelate, and is not worthy, his lamp quencheth anon. And

24

other men have told me that he that singeth the mass for the prelate that is dead, he shall find upon the altar the name written of him that shall be prelate chosen . . .

In that abbey entereth no fly, nor toads nor newts, nor such foul venomous beasts, nor lice nor fleas, by the miracle of God, and of our Lady. For there wont to be so many such manner of filths that the monks were in will to leave the place and the abbey, and were gone from thence upon the mountain above to eschew that place; and our Lady came to them and bade them turn again, and from thence forwards never entered such filth in that place amongst them, nor never shall enter hereafter. Also, before the gate is the well where Moses smote the stone of the which the water came out plenteously.

From Mount Sinai to Hebron, and to a legend going back at least to the time of Constantine, the first Christian emperor of Rome.

The Dry Tree

And a little from Hebron is the mount of Mamre, of the which the valley taketh its name. And there is a tree of oak that is of Abraham's time; the which men call the Dry Tree. And they say that it hath been there since the beginning of the world, and was some-time green and bare leaves, unto the time that our Lord died on the cross, and then it dried: and so did all the trees that were then in the world. And some say, by their prophecies, that a lord, a prince of the west side of the world, shall win the Land of Promise that is the Holy Land with help of Christian men, and he shall let sing a mass under that dry tree; and then the tree shall wax green and bear both fruit and leaves, and through that miracle many Saracens and Jews shall be turned to Christian faith: and therefore they do great worship thereto, and keep it full busily. And, albeit so, that it be dry, nevertheless yet it beareth great virtue, for certainly he that hath a little thereof upon him, it healeth him of the falling evil [epilepsy], and his horse shall not be afoundered: and many other virtues it hath; wherefore men hold it full precious.

There follows a story that may be even older. The name, Field Floridus, was also given to the Garden of Gethsemane.

How Roses Came first into the World

From Hebron men go to Bethlehem in half a day, for it is but five mile; and it is full fair way, by plains and woods full delectable. Bethlehem is a little city, long and narrow and well walled, and in each side enclosed with good ditches. And toward the east end of the city is a full fair church and a gracious, and it hath many towers, pinnacles and corners, full strong and curiously made; and within that church be forty-four pillars of marble, great and fair.

And between the city and the church is the field *Floridus*, that is to say, the 'field flourished'. For as much as a fair maiden was blamed with wrong, and slandered that she had done fornication; for which cause she was condemned to death, and to be burnt in that place, to the which she was led. And, as the fire began to burn about her, she made her prayers to our Lord, saying that she was not guilty of that sin, and praying that he would help her and make it to be known to all men, of his merciful grace. And when she had thus said she entered into the fire, and anon was the fire quenched and went out; and the brands that were burning became red rose-trees, and the brands that were not kindled became white rose-trees, full of roses. And these were the first rose-trees and roses, both white and red, that ever any man saw; and thus was this maiden saved by the grace of God. And therefore is that field named the field of God flourished, for it was full of roses.

The Church of the Holy Sepulchre in Jerusalem

And ye shall understand that when men come to Jerusalem, their first pilgrimage is to the Church of the Holy Sepulchre where Our Lord was buried, that is without the city on the north side; but it is now enclosed in with the town wall . . . And in the midst of the church is a tabernacle, as it were a little house, made with a low little door. And in the right side of that tabernacle is the sepulchre of Our Lord.

And in midst of that church is a compass [space], in the which Joseph of Arimathea laid the body of Our Lord when he had taken him down off the cross; and there he washed the wounds of Our Lord. And that compass, say men, is the midst of the world . . .

And from the Church of the Sepulchre, toward the east, at eight score paces, is *Templus Domini* [The Temple of our Lord]. It is a right fair house, and it is all round and high and covered with lead. And it is well paved with white marble. But the Saracens will not suffer no Christian man nor Jews to come therein, for they say that none so foul and sinful men should come in so holy place: but I came in there and in other places where I would, for I had letters of the soldan with his great seal, and commonly other men have but his signet. In the which letters he commanded, of his special grace, to all his subjects to let me see all the places, and to inform me plainly all the mysteries of every place, and to conduct me from city to city, if it were need, and buxomly to receive me and my company, and for to obey to all my requests reasonable if they were not greatly against the royal power and dignity of the soldan or of his law.

Another personal aside. We are told nothing about Mandeville's 'company'. It is worth recalling at this point that his book was a work of imagination and poetry, not a guide-book, a history or a geography, however anxious he may have been to persuade his readers of the contrary. When he ventures upon matters of fact he is pretty sure to go wrong.

The reader is now treated to a wonderful garbling of history. Mandeville tells of Julian the Apostate, the Roman emperor (r. AD 361–3) who reverted to paganism and, abominating Christians, gave the Jews leave to build a Jewish temple at Ierusalem. 'And when the Jews had made the temple, came an earthquaking, and cast it down (as God would) and destroyed all that they had made.' Later, says Mandeville, this temple was rebuilt, 'in the same manner as Solomon made it', by a Roman emperor whom he calls Adrian: 'And he would suffer no Jews to dwell there, but only Christian men. For although he was not christened yet he loved Christian men more than any nation save his own.'

For 'Adrian' read Hadrian, who, whether or not he had any particular affection for the Christians (a relatively unimportant sect in his day) was certainly a great emperor, an enlightened and tolerant man. But Hadrian reigned over Rome from AD 117 to 138, more than two centuries before Julian the Apostate. As for the earthquake, it occurred in the year 1114. The Church of the Holy Sepulchre, the greatest shrine in Christendom, was rebuilt by the Crusaders.

The church is described in detail but not altogether accurately, and this is followed by a number of Old Testament stories – the Ark of the Covenant, Jacob's Ladder and others. Then we have a very gruesome matter.

King Herod

And fast by is King Herod's house, that let slay the innocents. This Herod was over-much cursed and cruel. For first he let slay his wife that he loved right well; and for the passing love that he had to her when he saw her dead, he fell in a rage and out of his mind a great while. And he let slay his two sons that he had of that wife. And after that he let slay another of his wives and a son that he had with her. And after that he let slay his own mother; and he would have slain his brother also, but he died suddenly. And after he fell into sickness; and when he felt that he should die, he sent for his sister and all the lords of his land; and when they were come he let command them [sent them] to prison. And then he said to his sister, he knew well that men of the country would make no sorrow for his death; and therefore he made his sister swear that she should let smite off all the heads of the lords when he were dead; and then should all the land make sorrow for his death; and thus he made his testament. But his sister fulfilled not his will. For as soon as he was dead she delivered all the lords out of prison and let them go, each lord to his own, and told them all the purpose of her brother's ordinance. And so was this cursed king never made sorrow for, as he supposed for to have been.

Much is said about the River Jordan, for which Mandeville uses the word 'flome' (Latin *flumen*, a river).

About the flome Jordan be many churches where that many Christian men dwelled. And nigh thereto is the city of Ai that Joshua assailed and took. Also beyond the flome Jordan is the vale of Mamre, and that is a full fair vale. Also upon the hill that I spake of before, where our Lord fasted forty days, a two mile long from Galilee, is a fair hill and an high, where the enemy the fiend bare our Lord the third time to tempt him, and shewed him all the regions of the world and said, *Hic omnia tibi dabo, si cadens adoraveris me*; that is to say, 'All this shall I give thee, if thou fall and worship me.'

Also from the Dead Sea to go eastward, out of the marches of the Holy Land that is called the Land of Promission [promise], is a strong castle and fair on a hill that is called Carak in Sarmois; that is to say, Royally. That castle let make King Baldwin, that was king of France, when he had conquered that land and put it into Christian men's hands for to keep that country; and for that cause was it called the Mount Royal. And under it there is a town called Sobach, and there all about dwell Christian men under tribute.

This King Baldwin, or Baudouin, was never King of France. He was a brother of Godefroie de Bouillon, the leader of the First Crusade, whom he succeeded in 1100 as King of Jerusalem, after the city and its surrounding country had fallen to the crusaders. The nine crusades were spread over a period of nearly two centuries. The end came with the Christian defeat at Acre in 1291, only thirty years before Mandeville set out on his travels. The whole vast region of the Middle East and Asia Minor, with its population of Arabs, Jews, Egyptians, Syrians and Turks, passed under Moslem, predominantly Turkish, rule, having for a time been overrun by the Mongols. But Christian colonies (mainly Greek and commercial, and by no means all favourable to the crusaders) had existed in various parts of the country long before the crusades, and many remained after the business was over, living 'under tribute' as Mandeville says. The loss of the Holy Places occasioned widespread propaganda in favour of a tenth crusade for their recovery, and Mandeville was not unaffected by this. That it never happened was due largely to the fact that the Moslems, having to some extent reconciled their racial difficulties, had grown too strong; and also, the French, always the mainstay of the crusades, were seriously weakened by the Hundred Years' War. The story moves on, by way of the country of the Samaritans, to Nazareth.

Nazareth

After go men by the hill beside the plains of Galilee unto Nazareth, where was wont to be a great city and a fair; but now there is nought but a little village, and houses abroad here and there. And it is not walled. And it sits in a little valley, and there be hills all about. There was our Lady born, but she was gotten at Jerusalem. And because that our Lady was born at Nazareth, therefore bare our Lord his surname of that town. There took Joseph our Lady to wife, when she was fourteen year of age. And there Gabriel greeted our Lady, saying, *Ave gratis plena, Dominus tecum!* that is to say, 'Hail, full of grace, our Lord is with thee!' And this salutation was done in a place of a great altar of a fair church that was wont to be sometime [once stood there], but it is now all down, and men have made a little receipt [collecting office] beside a pillar of that church to receive the offerings of pilgrims. And the Saracens keep that place full dearly, for the profit that they have thereof. And they be full wicked Saracens and cruel, and more despiteful than in any other place, and have destroyed all the churches. There nigh is Gabriel's Well, where our Lord was wont to bathe him when he was young, and from that well bare he water often-time to his mother. And in that well she washed often-time the clouts of her Son Jesu Christ. And from Jerusalem thither is three journeys. At Nazareth was our Lord nourished. Nazareth is as much as to say, 'Flower of the garden', and rightly may it be called flower, for there was nourished the flower of life that was Christ Jesu.

Travelling into Syria Mandeville is struck by the use they make of carrier pigeons (culvers), although this can scarcely have been a novelty.

In that country and other countries beyond they have a custom, when they are at war, and when men hold siege about city or castle, and they within dare not send out messengers with letters from lord to lord for to ask succour, they make their letters and bind them to the neck of a culver, and let the culver flee. And the culvers be so taught, that they flee with those letters to the very place that men would send them to. For the culvers be nourished in those places where they be sent to, and they send them thus, for to bear their letters. And the culvers return again to the place where they be nourished; and so they do commonly.

There follows a description of the various Christian sects, with their different modes of worship, after which we come to the city of Damascus.

Damascus. Our Lady of Sardenak. The river Sabatory

That is a full fair city and full noble, and full of all merchandises, and three days' journey from the sea and five days from Jerusalem. But upon camels, mules, horses, dromedaries and other beasts, men carry their merchandise thither. And thither come the merchants with merchandise by sea from India, Persia, Chaldea, Armenia and many other kingdoms . . .

From Damascus men come again by our Lady of Sardenak, that is five mile from Damascus. And it sitteth upon a rock, and it is a full fair place; and it seemeth a castle, for there was once a castle, but it is now a full fair church. And there within be monks and nuns Christian. And there is a vault under the church where that Christian men dwell also. And they have many good vines. And in the church, behind the high altar, in the wall, is a table of black wood, on the which sometime was painted an image of our Lady that turneth into flesh: but now the image sheweth but little, but always, by the grace of God, that table evermore drops oil, as it were of olive; and there is a vessel of marble under the table to receive the oil. Thereof they give to pilgrims, for it heals of many sicknesses; and men say that if it be kept well seven year, afterwards it turns into flesh and blood . . .

Between the city of Arkaz and the city of Raphane is a river that is called Sabatory; for on a Saturday it runs fast, and all the week else it stands still and runs not, or else but fairly.

We shall later meet with another of these eccentric rivers. But now Mandeville turns to a subject which profoundly interests him. After describing the ways in which a traveller from the west may come to the Holy Land, and warning pilgrims of the difficulties and dangers of the journey, he discusses the religious beliefs of the Saracens (Moslems), according to 'the book Mohammed took them' – that is to say, the *Koran*, which he calls *Alkaron*.

Moslems and Christians

In the which book, among other things, is written, as I have often-times seen and read, that the good shall go to paradise and the evil to hell; and that believe all Saracens. And if a man ask them what paradise they mean, they say, to paradise that is a place of delights where men shall find all manner of fruits in all seasons, and rivers running of milk and honey, and of wine and of sweet water; and that they shall have fair houses and noble, every man after his desert, made of precious stones and of gold and of silver; and that every man shall have four score wives all maidens.

Also they believe and speak gladly of the Virgin Mary and of the Incarnation. And they say that Mary was taught of the angel; and that Gabriel said to her that she was for-chosen from the beginning of the world; and that he shewed to her the Incarnation of Jesu Christ; and that she conceived and bare child maiden; and that witnesseth their book.

And they say also that when the angel shewed the Incarnation of Christ unto Mary, she was young and had great dread. For there was then an enchanter in the country that dealt with witchcraft, that men called Taknia, that by his enchantments could make him in likeness of an angel, and went often-times and lay with maidens. And therefore Mary dreaded lest it had been Taknia, that came for to deceive the maidens. And therefore she conjured the angel that he should tell her if it were he or no. And the angel answered and said that she should have no dread of him, for he was very messenger of Jesu Christ. Also their book saith that when that she had childed under a palm tree she had great shame that she had a child; and she grieved and said that she would that she had been dead. And anon the child spake to her and comforted her, and said, 'Mother, dismay thee nought, for God hath hid in thee his privities for the salvation of the world.' And in other many places saith their Alkaron that Jesu Christ spake as soon as he was born. And that book saith also that Jesu was sent from God Almighty for to be mirror and example and token to all men.

And the Alkaron saith also of the day of doom how God shall come to doom all manner of folk. And the good he shall draw on his side and put them into bliss, and the wicked he shall condemn to the pains of hell. And among all prophets Jesu was the most excellent and the most worthy next God, and that he made the gospels in the which is good doctrine and healthful, full of clarity and soothfastness and true preaching to them that believe in God. And he was a very prophet and more than a prophet, and lived without sin, and gave sight to the blind, and healed the lepers, and raised dead men, and ascended to heaven.

Jesus of Nazareth was second only to Mohammed himself in the Moslem canon of great holy men. This was one reason why, despite all differences of doctrine, the Moslems tolerated the presence of Christians among them; but we need not doubt that commerce was also a large consideration.

The passage that follows must be accepted as fiction. Using the device of the 'imaginary conversation', which was no rarity then or later, Mandeville proceeds to air his views on current Christian morality and conduct, severely castigating his fellow-Christians. What he says would doubtless have been echoed by many cultivated Moslems (Christians too, for that matter), although the former would have been unlikely to agree that the Christians had only to mend their ways to reconquer the Holy Land. It has been suggested that Mandeville was here adding his voice to the clamour for a tenth Crusade (as he may also have been doing in the story of the Dry Tree). In any event, we may admire the skill of his performance, the artful build-up and the impressive account of the Sultan's intelligence service.

And therefore I shall tell you what the soldan told me upon a day in his chamber. He sent out of his chamber all manner of men, lords and others, for he would speak with me in counsel. And there he asked me how the Christian men governed them in our country. And I said him, 'Right well, thanked be God!'

And he said me, 'Truly nay! For ye Christian men care not how untruly ye serve God! Ye should give example to the lewd [ignorant] people for to do well, and ye give them example to do evil. For the common people, upon festival days, when they should go to church to serve God, then go they to taverns and be there in gluttony all the day and all night, and eat and drink as beasts that have no reason and know not when they have enough. And also the Christian men enforce themselves, in all manners that they may, for to fight and for to deceive one another. And therewithal they be so proud that they know not how to be clothed; now long, now short, now strait, now large, now sworded, now daggered, and in all manner of guises. They should be simple, meek and true and full of charity, as Jesu was, in whom they believe; but they be all the contrary, and ever inclined to the evil and to do evil. And they be so covetous that for a little silver they sell their daughters, their sisters and their own wives to put them to lechery. And one withdraweth the wife of another, and none of them holdeth faith to another; but they defoul their law that Jesu Christ betook them to keep for their salvation. And thus for their sins have they lost all this land that we hold. For, for their sins, their God hath taken this country into our hands, not only by strength of ourself, but for their sins. For we know well, in very sooth, that when ye serve God, God will help you; and when he is with you, no man may be against you. And that know we well by our prophecies, that Christian men shall win again this land out of our hands, when they serve God more devoutly; but as long as they be of foul and of unclean living (as they be now) we have no dread of them in no kind, for their God will not help them in no wise.'

And then I asked him how he knew the state of Christian men. And he answered me, that he knew all the state of all courts of Christian kings and

The Castle of the Sparrow hawk

The Well of Youth. Notice the men picking pepper at the foot of the mountain, and the old men coming to the Fountain of Youth.

princes, and the state of the common people also, by his messengers that he sent to all lands, in manner as they were merchants of precious stones, of cloths of gold and of other things, for to know the manner of every country amongst Christian men. And then he called in all the lords that he had sent out of his chamber, and there he shewed me four that were great lords in the country, that told me of my country and of many other Christian countries, as well as they had been of the same country; and they spake French right well, and the soldan also; whereof I had great marvel.

Alas! that it is great slander to our faith and to our law when folk that be without law shall reprove us and tell us of our sins, and they that should be converted to Christ and to the law of Jesu by our good example and by our acceptable life to God, be, through our wickedness and evil living, far from us and strangers and hold us for wicked livers and cursed. And truly they say sooth, for the Saracens be good and faithful; for they keep entirely the commandment of the holy book Alkaron that God sent them by his messenger Mahomet, to the which, as they say, Saint Gabriel the angel often-time told the will of God.

With this, and after some further account of Mohammed, Mandeville takes leave of the Holy Land and the affairs of the western world.

Chapter 3

TRAVELLING EASTWARD

The Castle of the Sparrow-hawk – Mount Ararat – Manna – The Land of the Amazons –
The Sciapods – A Discourse on Diamonds

HAVING TAKEN his readers through the Holy Land, 'Now is time, if it like you,'
says Mandeville, 'to tell of the countries beyond.'

For in those countries beyond be many diverse countries and many great
kingdoms, that be departed [separated] by the four floods that come from
Paradise Terrestrial. For Mesopotamia and the kingdom of Chaldea and
Arabia be between the two rivers of Tigris and of Euphrates; and the kingdom of Media and of Persia be between the rivers of Nile and of Tigris; and
the kingdom of Syria, whereof I have spoken before, and Palestine and
Phoenicia be between Euphrates and the sea Mediterranean, the which sea
dureth in length from Morocco, upon the sea of Spain, unto the Great Sea.

The Mediterranean itself was commonly referred to as the 'Great Sea'. But in
view of what is to come it looks as though Mandeville, ignoring the isthmus of
Suez, is here including the Indian Ocean in a boundless expanse of waters enclosing
the uncharted regions of Ind and Cathay. The geography, in any event, now becomes very strange. There is mention of the Caspian Sea and of Amazonia, which
we return to later, followed by an abrupt descent into Africa.

In that country of Lybia (that is to say, Lybia the low) that beginneth at the
sea of Spain where the Pillars of Hercules be, and endureth unto Egypt and
toward Ethiopia – in that country is the sea more high than the land, yet it
passeth not its marks. And whoso turneth toward the east, the shadow of
himself is on the right side; and here, in our country, the shadow is on the
left side. In that sea of Lybia is no fish; for they may not live for the great heat
of the sun, because that the water is evermore boiling. And many other lands
there be that it were too long to tell or to number. But of some parts I shall
speak more plainly hereafter.

That continuously boiling sea, which seems to have been situated somewhere
south of the equator, is an unexplained mystery. We go north to Trebizond (or

34

Trabson) on the Black Sea, and thence to Little Armenia, where there is a famous tale to tell.

Of the Wishings for Watching of the Sparrow-hawk

And in that country is an old castle that stands upon a rock, the which is called the castle of the Sparrow-hawk; where men find a sparrow-hawk upon a perch right fair and right well made, and a fair lady of faerie that keepeth it. And who that will watch that sparrow-hawk seven days and seven nights, or, as some men say, three days and three nights, without company and without sleep, that fair lady shall give him, when he hath done, the first wish that he will wish of earthly things; and that hath been proved often-times.

And one time befell, that a King of Armenia, that was a worthy knight and doughty man, and a noble prince, watched that hawk some time. And at the end of seven days and seven nights the lady came to him and bade him wish, for he had well deserved it. And he answered that he was great lord enough, and well in peace, and had enough of worldly riches; and therefore he would wish none other thing but the body of that fair lady, to have it at his will. And she answered him that he knew not what he asked, and said that he was a fool to desire what he might not have; for she said that he should not ask but for earthly things, for she was none earthly thing, but a ghostly thing. And the king said that he would ask none other thing. And the lady answered: 'Since that I may not withdraw you from your lewd desire, I shall give you without wishing, and to all them that shall come of you. Sir King! ye shall have war without peace, and always to the nine degree, ye shall be in subjection of your enemies, and ye shall be needy of all goods.' And never since, neither the King of Armenia nor the country were in peace nor had they ever plenty of goods; and they have been always under tribute of the Saracens.

Also the son of a poor man watched that hawk and wished that he might chieve well [succeed in life]; and to be happy to merchandise. And the lady granted his wish. And he became the most rich and the most famous merchant that might be on sea or on earth. And he became so rich that he knew not the thousand part of that he had. And he was wiser in wishing than was the king.

Through Turkey to Erzerum and thence to Mount Ararat, where Noah's Ark came to rest when the Flood subsided, and where, Mandeville tells us, it was still visible.

The Ark

And men may see it afar in clear weather. And that mountain is well a seven mile high. And some men say that they have seen and touched the ship, and put their fingers in the parts where the fiend went out, when that Noah said, Benedicite. But they that say such words, say their will [what they would like to believe]. For a man may not go up the mountain, for great plenty of snow that is always on that mountain, neither summer nor winter. So that no man may go up there, nor ever man did since the time of Noah, save a monk that, by the grace of God, brought one of the planks down, that yet is in the minster at the foot of the mountain.

And beside is the city of Dain that Noah founded. And fast by is the city of Any in the which were once a thousand churches.

Again the itinerary becomes vague. After passing through Persia we come to the land of Job, that sorely tried man whose patience eventually met with its reward, and thence to Chaldea. By Mandeville's account Job was even more richly rewarded than the Old Testament tells us, and he died at the age of 248.

In that land of Job there is no default of anything that is needful to man's body. There be hills where men get great plenty of manna, in greater abundance than in any other country. This manna is called bread of angels. And it is a white thing that is full sweet and right delicious, and more sweet than honey or sugar. And it cometh of the dew of heaven that falleth upon the herbs in that country. And it congealeth and becometh all white and sweet. And men put it in medicines for to make the womb lax, and to purge evil blood. For it cleanseth the blood and putteth out melancholy. This land of Job marcheth to the kingdom of Chaldea.

This land of Chaldea is full great. And the language of that country is more great in sounding than it is in other parts beyond the sea. Men pass to go beyond by the Tower of Babylon the Great [the Tower of Babel], where all the languages were first changed. And that is a four days' journey from Chaldea. In that realm be fair men, and they go full nobly arrayed in clothes of gold, embroidered and apparelled with great pearls and precious stones full nobly. And the women be right foul and evil arrayed. And they go all barefoot and clothed in evil garments large and wide, but they be short to the knees, and long sleeves down to the feet like a monk's frock, and their sleeves be hanging about their shoulders. And they be black women foul and hideous, and truly they are as evil as they be foul.

It seems decidedly odd that in a country where the men were so splendid (and fair) the women should have been so awful (and black). The problem is one that might have aroused Mandeville's scientific interest, but no explanation is offered. The next story is entirely to do with women – less repellent, we may suppose, than those ladies of Chaldea.

The Land of the Amazons

Beside the land of Chaldea is the land of Amazonia, that is the land of Feminye. And in that realm is all women and no man; not, as some men say, that men may not [cannot] live there, but because that the women will suffer no men amongst them to be their sovereigns.

For sometime there was a king in that country. And men married, as in other countries. And so befell that the king had war with them of Scythia, and he was slain in battle, and all the good blood of his realm. And when the queen and all the other noble ladies saw that they were all widows, and that all the royal blood was lost, they armed them and, being mad with grief, they slew all the men of the country that were left; for they would that all the women were widows as the queen and they were. And from that time hitherwards they never would suffer man to dwell amongst them longer than seven days and seven nights; nor that any male child should dwell amongst them longer than he were nourished; and then sent to his father. And when they will have any company of man then they draw them towards the lands marching next to them. And they dwell with them an eight days or ten, and then go home again. And if they have any boy child they keep it a certain time, and then send it to the father when he can go alone and eat by himself; or else they slay it. And if it be a female they do away with one breast. And if it be a woman of great lineage they do away the left breast that they may the better bear a shield. And if it be a woman on foot they do away the right breast, for to shoot with bow turkeys [Turkish bows]; for they shoot well with bows.

In that land they have a queen that governeth all that land, and all they be obeissant to her. And always they make her queen by election that is most worthy in arms; for they be right good warriors and wise, noble and worthy. And they go often-time to help of other kings in their wars, for gold and silver as other soldiers do; and they maintain themselves right vigorously. This land of Amazonia is an isle, all environed with the sea save in two places, where be two entries. And beyond that water dwell the men that be their loves, where they go to solace them when they will.

In the ancient legend, Theseus, King of Athens, the slayer of the Minotaur and the great hero of Attica, invaded the country of the Amazons and carried off their queen, Hippolyta (she is also called Antiope), whom he married. Shakespeare introduces Theseus and Hippolyta into his *Midsummer Night's Dream*, but Mandeville does not mention either. Strangely, his book contains almost no direct reference to the Greek myths, with which he must certainly have been familiar, as was every educated person in his day.

He now takes us back into Africa.

Ethiopia and the Sciapods

In Ethiopia all the rivers and all the waters be troubled, and they be somedeal salt for the great heat that is there. And the folk of that country be lightly drunken and have but little appetite to meat. And they have commonly the flux of the womb. And they live not long. In Ethiopia be many diverse folk; and Ethiope is called Cusis. In that country be folk that have but one foot, and they go so blyve [nimbly] that it is marvel. And the foot is so large that it shadoweth all the body against the sun, when they will lie and rest them. In Ethiopia, when the children be young and little, they be all yellow; and when that they wax of age, that yellowness turneth to be all black. In Ethiopia is the city of Saba, and the land of the which one of the three kings that presented our Lord in Bethlehem was king of.

The peculiar species or tribe termed Sciapods – people with a single foot so large that it could be used as a parasol if they lay on their backs – had already been heard of and was frequently drawn by medieval artists (there is a Sciapod in the *Mappa Mundi*). It is sad that Mandeville has so little to tell us about them. They are the first of the extraordinary array of creatures, human, part-human or monstrous, which contributed so largely at first to the popularity of his book, and eventually to its disrepute.

The story is approaching the land of Ind, concerning which Mandeville tells us that it was divided into three parts, one torrid, one temperate and one bitterly cold. But first there is a digression.

Whether or not Mandeville had any first-hand knowledge of diamonds, it is very clear that he shared the *mystique*, the strange spell, having little to do with rarity or commercial value, which diamonds have exercised upon mankind from the earliest antiquity. Their magical properties and the living quality which caused them to breed and grow like some form of sea or plant life – these ancient beliefs are here memorably expressed.

Discourse on Diamonds

Albeit that men find good diamonds in Ind, yet nevertheless men find them more commonly upon the rocks in the sea and upon hills where the mine of gold is. And there be some of the greatness of a bean and some as great as an hazel nut. And they be square and pointed of their own kind, both above and beneath, without working of man's hand. And they grow together, male and female. And they be nourished with the dew of heaven. And they engender commonly and bring forth small children, that multiply and grow all the year. I have often-times found that if a man keep them with a little of the rock and wet them with May-dew oft-sithes [often], they shall grow every year and the small will wax great. For right as the fine pearl congealeth and waxeth great of the dew of heaven, right so doth the very diamond; and right as the pearl of his own kind taketh roundness, so the diamond, by virtue of God, taketh squareness. And a man shall bear the diamond on his left side, for it is of greater virtue then than on the right side; for the strength of their growing is toward the north, that is the left side of the world, and the left part of man is when he turneth his face toward the east.

And if you like to know the virtues of the diamond, I shall tell you what they beyond the sea say and affirm, of whom all science and all philosophy cometh. He that beareth the diamond upon him, it giveth him hardiness and manhood, and it keepeth the limbs of his body whole. It giveth him victory of his enemies in plea [law-suit] and in war, if his cause be rightful. And it keepeth him that beareth it in good wit [of sound mind]. And it keepeth him from strife and riot, from ill-fortune, from sorrows and from enchantments, and from fantasies and illusions of wicked spirits. And if any cursed witch or enchanter would bewitch him that beareth the diamond, all that sorrow and mischance shall turn upon the enchanter through virtue of that stone. And also no wild beast dare assail the man that beareth it on him. Also the diamond should be given freely, without coveting and without buying, and then it is of greater virtue. And it maketh a man more strong and more sad against [compassionate to] his enemies. And it healeth him that is lunatic, and them that the fiend pursueth or travaileth. And if venom or poison be brought in presence of the diamond, anon it beginneth to wax moist and for to sweat.

I shall speak a little more of the diamonds, although I tarry my matter for a time, to the end that they that know them not be not deceived by gabbers that go by the country to sell them. For whoso will buy the diamond, it is needful to him that he know them. Because that men counterfeit them often

39

of crystal that is yellow, and of sapphires of citron colour that is yellow also, and of the sapphire loupe and of many other stones. But I tell you these counterfeits be not so hard; and also the points will break lightly, and men may easily polish them. But some workmen, for malice, will not polish them; to that intent to make men believe that they may not be polished. But men may try them in this manner. First cut with them or write with them on sapphires, on crystal or on other precious stones. After that, men take the adamant, that is the shipman's stone, that draweth the needle to itself, and men lay the diamond upon the adamant, and lay the needle before the adamant; and, if the diamond be good and virtuous, the adamant draweth not the needle whiles the diamond is there present. And this is the proof that they beyond the sea make.

Natheles it befalleth often-time that the good diamond loseth its virtue by sin, and for incontinence of him that beareth it. And then it is needful to make it to recover its virtue again, or else it is of little value.

That is to say, the owner of the diamond had to turn over a new leaf if it was not to lose its magic. The 'adamant' was lodestone, the magnetic rock that attracts metal and may divert the compasses of ships at sea, about which we shall hear more later. The notion that a genuine diamond, but nothing else, had the power to neutralise the lodestone's magnetism was another ancient belief.

'They beyond the sea . . .' The narrow meaning of 'beyond the sea' was *Outremer*, the countries where the crusades were fought; but Mandeville often uses the word 'beyond' in a far wider sense – beyond the oceans, beyond the bounds of Christendom, beyond our half of the world.

And so we come to the land of Ind.

Chapter 4

THE LAND OF IND

*The Growing of Pepper – The Well of Youth – The Judgements of St Thomas –
Juggernaut – The Isle of Lamary*

INDIA was still a land of mystery to the peoples of the west, and Mandeville's 'Ind'
is a vast, undefined region embracing not only the sub-continent itself (what little
was known of it) but extending beyond the Bay of Bengal to include the East
Indies and southern China. His piecemeal account is based on fables going back to
Alexander, whose great shadow pervades so much of his book, on scattered
travellers' tales, and on the more reliable but scanty report of the Franciscan
missionary, Friar Odoric. The general idea may be gathered from Mandeville's
opening lines.

In Ind be full many diverse countries. And it is called Ind, for a river that
runneth throughout the country [the Indus]. In that river men find eels of
thirty foot long and more. And the folk that dwell nigh that water be of evil
colour, green and yellow. In Ind and about Ind be more than 5000 isles good
and great that men dwell in, without not counting those that be [un]inhabit-
able, and without other small isles. In every isle is great plenty of cities and of
towns, and of folk without number. For men of Ind have this condition of
kind, that they never go out of their own country, and therefore is there
great multitude of people.

They were also, we are told, a people of many religions.

For some of them worship the sun, some the moon, some the fire, some
trees, some serpents, or the first thing that they meet at morrow. And some
worship simulacres and some idols. But between simulacres and idols is a
great difference. For simulacres be images made after likeness of men or of
women, or of the sun, or of the moon, or of any beast, or of any kindly thing.
And idols is an image made of lewd will of man, that man may not find
among kindly things, as an image that hath four heads, one of a man,
another of an horse or of an ox, or of some other beast that no man hath seen
after kindly disposition.

Going mainly by sea, from island to island, the traveller comes to 'the land of Lomb' where pepper was grown 'in a vast forest called Combar, eighteen days' journey across'. This land of Lomb can only have been in the East Indies, since pepper in those days grew nowhere else.

The Growing of Pepper

And ye shall understand, that the pepper groweth in manner as doth a wild vine that is planted fast by the trees of that wood for to sustain it by, as doth the vine. And the fruit thereof hangeth in manner as raisins. And the tree is so thick charged that it seemeth that it would break. And when it is ripe it is all green, as it were ivy berries. And then men cut them, as men do the vines, and then they put it upon an oven, and there it waxeth black and crisp . . .

In that country be many manner serpents and of other vermin for the great heat of the country and of the pepper. And some men say that when they will gather the pepper they make fire, and burn about to make the serpents and the cockodrills [crocodiles] to flee. But save their grace [with respect] this cannot be so. For if they burnt about the trees that bear, the pepper would be burnt, and it would dry up all the virtue, as of any other thing; and they would never quench the fire. But thus they do: they anoint their hands and their feet with a juice made of snails and of other things of the which the serpents and the venomous beasts hate and dread the savour; and that maketh them flee before them, because of the smell, and then they gather it safely enough.

There was a mountain at the edge of that pepper-forest. Alas, we are given no clue to its exact location.

The Well of Youth

And at the foot of that mount is a fair well and a great, that hath odour and savour of all spices. And at every hour of the day it changeth its odour and its savour diversely. And whoso drinketh three times fasting of the water of that well he is whole of all manner of sickness that he hath. And they that dwell there and drink often of that well, they never have sickness; and they seem always young. I have drunken thereof three or four times, and me-thinketh I fare the better. Some men call it the well of youth. For they that often drink thereof seem always young-like, and live without sickness. And men say, that that well cometh out of paradise, and therefore it is so virtuous.

Many tales were told of the Well or Fountain of Youth. It was said, for example, that those who drank from it need do so only three times in every hundred years and they would live to be 500 years old, always in perfect health. Mandeville, drawing on various sources (principally the letter of Prester John) might have made a much better story of it if he had been able to resist the temptation to tell the reader that he himself had drunk the water. Why, in this case, did he so rapidly become an old man suffering from 'gouts artetykes', as he tells us at the end of his book? He could only play the whole thing down and pass rapidly on to safer topics. His next sentence runs:

'By all that country groweth good ginger, and therefore thither go the merchants for spicery.'

Back in India proper, Mandeville turns to the religious customs of the Hindus. Here he had recourse to known sources, and many of the places can be identified.

In that land men worship the ox for his simpleness and for his meekness, and for the profit that cometh of him. And they say, that he is the holiest beast in earth. For them seemeth, that whosoever be meek and patient, he is holy and profitable; for then, they say, he hath all virtue in him. They make the ox to labour six year or seven, and then they eat him.

And when any man dieth in the country they burn his body in name of penance; to that intent, that he suffer no pain in earth to be eaten of worms. And if his wife have no child they burn her with him, and say that it is reason that she make him company in that other world as she did in this. But if she have children by him, they let her live with them, to bring them up if she will. And if that she love more to live with her children than for to die with her husband, men hold her for false and cursed; she shall never be loved nor trusted of the people. And if the woman die before the husband, men burn him with her, if that he will. And if he will not, no man constraineth him thereto, but he may wed another time without blame or reproof.

In that country grow many strong vines. And the women drink wine, and men not. And the women shave their beards, and the men not.

The Hindu practice of suttee (the burning of the wife or wives alive on the husband's funeral pyre) was only suppressed by the British in the nineteenth century. We move on, ten days' journey, to a country called Mabaron (the coast of Coromandel), 'a great kingdom, and it hath many fair cities and towns.'

The Judgements of St Thomas

In that kingdom lieth the body of Saint Thomas the apostle in flesh and bone, in a fair tomb in the city of Calamye [Mailapur]; for there he was martyred and buried. And men of Assyria bare his body into Mesopotamia into the city of Edessa, and later he was brought thither again. And the arm and the hand that he put in our Lord's side, when He appeared to him after His resurrection and said to him, *Noli esse incredulus, sed fidelis* [Do not be unbelieving but faithful] is yet lying in a vessel without the tomb. And by that hand they make all their judgements in the country, whoso hath right or wrong. For when there is any dissension between two parties, and each of them maintaineth his cause, and saith that his cause is rightful, and the other saith the contrary, then both parties write their causes in two bills and put them in the hand of Saint Thomas. And anon he casteth away the bill of the wrong cause and holdeth still the bill with the right cause. And therefore men come from far countries to have judgement of doubtable causes. And other judgement use they none there.

Also the church, where Saint Thomas lieth, is both great and fair, and all full of great simulacres, and those be great images that they call their gods, of the which the least is as great as two men.

This St Thomas was the apostle Thomas Didymus, 'doubting Thomas'. Early tradition had it that he was buried in Edessa, as Mandeville says; but a later story, that he preached in India (possibly founding the Christian order of St Thomas of Malabar) came to be generally accepted.

The story that follows is founded directly on fact. The temple of the god Jaganath (or Juggernaut, as the British were later to call him) was, and is, in the town of Puri on the east coast of India, one of the most ancient of Indian religious centres and still a place of pilgrimage. The ceremony of dragging the enormous car (forty-five feet high, with sixteen wheels seven feet in diameter) carrying the god's idol through the streets of the town is still repeated every year, although in these days sacrificial victims do not commonly fling themselves beneath its wheels.

Juggernaut

And, amongst these other, there is a great image more [larger] than any of the other, that is all covered with fine gold and precious stones and rich pearls; and that idol is the god of false Christians that have denied their faith. And it sitteth in a chair of gold, full nobly arrayed, and he hath about his neck large girdles wrought of gold and precious stones and pearls. And this church is full richly wrought and all overgilt within. And to that idol go men on pilgrimage, as commonly and with as great devotion as Christian men go to Saint James [at Compostela], or other holy pilgrimages. And many folk that come from far lands to seek that idol for the great devotion that they have, they look never upward but evermore down to the earth, for dread to see anything about them that should let them of their devotion. And some there be that go on pilgrimage to this idol bearing knives in their hands that be made full keen and sharp; and always as they go they smite themselves in their arms and in their legs and in their thighs with many hideous wounds; and so they shed their blood for love of that idol.

And before the minster of this idol is a vivary, in manner of a great lake, full of water. And therein pilgrims cast gold and silver, pearls and precious stones without number, instead of offerings. And when the ministers of that church need to make any reparation of the church or of any of the idols, they take gold and silver, pearls and precious stones out of the vivary, to quit the costage of such things as they make or repair; so that nothing is faulty but anon it shall be amended. And ye shall understand that when there be great feasts and solemnities of that idol, as the dedication of the church and the throning of the idol, all the country about meet there together. And they set this idol upon a car with great reverence, well arrayed with cloths of gold, of rich cloths of Tartary, of Samake [samite] and other precious cloths. And they lead him about the city with great solemnity. And before the car go first in procession all the maidens of the country, two and two together full ordinately. And after those maidens go the pilgrims. And some of them fall down under the wheels of the car and let the car go over them, so that they be dead anon. And some have their arms or their limbs all broken, and some the sides. And all this do they for love of their god, in great devotion. And they thinketh that the more pain and the more tribulation that they suffer for love of their god, the more joy they shall have in another world. And, shortly to say you, they suffer so great pains, and so hard martyrdoms for love of their idol, that a Christian man, I trow, durst not take upon him the tenth part the pain for love of our Lord Jesu Christ. And after, I say you, before the car, go all the minstrels of the country without number, with diverse instruments, and they make all the melody that they can.

The self-inflicted religious torments of the Hindus were numerous and horrifying. We may pass on to a matter which, in part at least, is no less deplorable. The title is Mandeville's own. But although he disapproved of the primitive people of Lamary (Sumatra) it was their cannibalism that really shocked his tolerant mind, far more than their state of naked communism.

The Evil Customs used in the Isle of Lamary

From that country go men by the sea ocean, and by many divers isles and by many countries that were too long for to tell of. And fifty-two days' journey from this land that I have spoken of, there is another land that is full great, that men call Lamary. In that land is full great heat. And the custom there is such, that men and women go all naked. And they scorn when they see any strange folk going clothed. And they say that God made Adam and Eve all naked, and that no man should shame him to shew him such as God made him, for nothing is foul that is of kindly nature. And they say that they that be clothed be folk of another world, or they be folk that trow not in God. And they say that they believe in God that formed the world, and that made Adam and Eve and all other things. And they wed there no wives, for all the women there be common and they forsake no man. And they say they sin if they refuse any man. And so God commanded to Adam and Eve and to all that come of him, when he said, *Crescite et multiplicamini et replete terram.* [Be fruitful and multiply, and replenish the earth.] And therefore may no man in that country say, This is my wife; nor no woman may say, This my husband. And when they have children, they may give them to what man they will that hath companied with them. And also all the land is common; for all that a man holdeth one year, another man hath it another year; and every man taketh what part that him liketh. And also all the goods of the land be common, corn and all other things: for nothing there is kept in close, nor nothing there is under lock, and every man there taketh what he will without any contradiction, and as rich is one man there as is another.

But in that country there is a cursed custom, for they eat more gladly man's flesh than any other flesh; and yet is that country abundant of flesh, of fish, of corns, of gold and silver and of all other goods. Thither go merchants and bring with them children to sell to them of the country, and they buy them. And if they be fat they eat them anon. And if they be lean they feed them till they be fat, and then they eat them. And they say that it is the best flesh and the sweetest of all the world.

And here, attached for no reason to the account of the Island of Lamary, there follows the largest and most important of the book's several digressions, Mandeville's argument that the earth is round, not flat. Since it does nothing to further the story and is moreover a matter of some intricacy, couched in the scientific language of the time, we have removed it from the main body of this volume and transferred it to the Appendix, where it is reproduced intact for the benefit of the reader who may be disposed to examine it.

Chapter 5

MANY ISLANDS

Java – The Island of Strange Trees – The Island of Elephants, Fishes and Snails – The Island of Cave-dwellers – The Dog-people – The Island of Cockodrills and the Tears of Adam and Eve – Strange Inhabitants of the Islands round Dondun – The Kingdom of Mancy – The Garden of Beasts – The Land of Pigmies

THE STORY now travels amid the '5,000 islands' of Mandeville's Ind, moving, in fact, by way of the East Indies to southern China; and since it has now passed safely beyond the bounds of the known world, penetrating deep into regions of fabulous rumour and report, no marvel is too great for it.

Java

A great isle and a great country that is nigh two thousand mile in circuit. And the king of that country is a full great lord and a rich and a mighty, and hath under him seven other kings of seven other isles about him. This isle is full well inhabited, and full well manned. There grow all manner of spicery, more plenteously than in any other country, as of ginger, cloves-gilogre, canell [cinnamon], seedwell, nutmegs and maces. Many other spices and many other goods grow in that isle. For of all things is there plenty, save only of wine. But there is gold and silver, great plenty. And the king of that country hath a palace full noble and full marvellous, and more rich than any in the world. For all the degrees [stair-treads] to go up into halls and chambers be, one of gold, another of silver. And also, the pavements of halls and chambers be all square, of gold one, and another of silver. And wit well, that the king of that isle is so mighty that he hath many times overcome the great Chan of Cathay in battle, that is the most great emperor that is under the firmament either beyond the sea or on this half [hemisphere]. For they have had often-time war between them, because that the great Chan would constrain him to hold his land of him; but the other at all times defendeth him well against him.

The Island of Strange Trees

After that isle, in going by sea, men find another isle, good and great, that men call Pathen, that is a great kingdom full of fair cities and full of towns. In that land grow trees that bear meal, whereof men make good bread and white and of good savour; and it seemeth as it were of wheat, but it is not allinges [wholly] of such savour. And there be other trees that bear honey good and sweet, and other trees that bear venom, against the which there is no medicine but one; and that is to take their proper leaves and stamp them and temper them with water and then drink it, or else he shall die; for balm will not avail, nor any other medicine. And other trees there be also that bear wine of noble sentiment. And if you like to hear how the meal cometh out of the trees I shall say you. Man hew the trees with an hatchet, all about the foot of the tree, till that the bark be parted in many parts, and then cometh out thereof a thick liquor, the which they receive in vessels, and dry it at the heat of the sun; and then they have it to a mill to grind and it becometh fair meal and white. And the honey and the wine and the venom be drawn out of other trees in the same manner, and put in vessels for to keep.

The Island of Elephants and Fishes

After this isle men go by sea to another isle that is called Calonak. And it is a fair land and a plenteous of goods. And the king of that country hath as many wives as he will. For he maketh search all the country to get him the fairest maidens that may be found, and maketh them to be brought before him. And he taketh one one night, and another another night, and so forth continually, so that he hath a thousand wives or more. And therefore the king getteth full many children, some-time an hundred, some-time a two-hundred, and some-time more. And he hath also 14,000 elephants or more that he maketh for to be brought up amongst his villains [serfs] by all his towns. For in case that he hath any war against any other king about him, then he maketh certain men of arms for to go up into the castles of wood made for war, that craftily be set upon the elephants' backs, for to fight against their enemies. And so do other kings there-about. For the manner of war is not there as it is here or in other countries, nor the ordinance of war neither.

And in that isle there is a great marvel, more to speak of than in any other part of the world. For all manner of fishes, that be there in the sea about them, come once in the year – each manner of diverse fishes, one manner of kind

Elephants with castles of wood made for war set upon their backs

The Dog-People

after other. And they cast themselves to the sea bank of that isle in so great plenty and multitude, that a man may unnethe [scarcely] see but fish. And there they abide three days. And every man of the country taketh of them as many as him liketh. And after the third day that manner of fish departeth and goeth into the sea. And after them come another multitude of fish of another kind and do in the same manner as the first did, other three days. And after them another, till all the diverse manner of fishes have been there, and that men have taken of them that them liketh. And no man knoweth the cause wherefore it may be. I know not the reason why it is, but God knoweth; but this, meseemeth, is the most marvel that ever I saw, that the fishes that have freedom to environ all the coasts of the sea at their own list, come of their own will to proffer them to the death, without constraining of man.

Mandeville was evidently no fisherman or he would have known that this 'great marvel' was nothing more remarkable than the annual spawning run of some variety of fish. It is strange that a phenomenon so commonplace should have so greatly astonished him.

The Island of Cave-Dwellers

Men go by sea, from isle to isle, unto an isle that is called Tracoda, where the folk of that country be as beasts, and unreasonable, and dwell in caves that they make in the earth; for they have no wit to make them houses. And when they see any man passing through their countries they hide them in their caves. And they eat flesh of serpents, and they eat but little. And they speak nought, but they hiss as serpents do. And they set no price by possessions or riches, but only by a precious stone that is amongst them, that is of sixty colours. And they love more that stone than anything else; and yet they know not the virtue thereof, but they covet it and love it only for its beauty.

The Dog-People

After that isle men go by the sea ocean, by many isles, unto an isle that is called Nacumera, that is a great isle and good and fair. And it is in compass about more than a thousand mile. And all the men and women of that isle have hounds' heads, and they be called Cynoceptales. And they be full reasonable and of good understanding, save that they worship an ox for their God. And also every one of them beareth an ox of gold or of silver in his forehead, in token that they love well their God. And they go all naked save a little clout. They be great folk and well-fighting. And they have a great targe [shield] that covereth all the body, and a spear in their hand to fight with. And if they take any man in battle, anon they eat him.

The Island of Cockodrills and the Tears of Adam and Eve

From this land men go to another isle that is called Silha. And it is well an 800 miles about. In that land is full much waste, for it is full of serpents, of dragons and of cockodrills, that no man dare dwell there. These cockodrills [crocodiles] be serpents, yellow and rayed above, and have four feet and short thighs, and great nails as claws or talons. And there be some that have five fathoms in length, and some of six and of eight and of ten. And when they go by places that be gravelly, it seemeth as though men had drawn a great tree through the gravelly place. And there be also many wild beasts, and namely of elephants.

In that isle is a great mountain. And in mid place of the mount is a great lake in a full fair plain; and there is great plenty of water. And they of the country say that Adam and Eve wept upon that mount a hundred year when they were driven out of Paradise, and the water, they say, is of their tears; for so much water they wept, that they made the foresaid lake. And in the bottom of that lake men find many precious stones and great pearls. In that lake grow many reeds and great canes; and there within be many cockodrills and serpents and great water-leeches. And the king of that country, once every year, giveth leave to poor men to go into the lake to gather them precious stones and pearls, by way of alms, for the love of God that made Adam . . .

In that country and others there-about there be wild geese that have two heads. And there be lions, all white and as great as oxen, and many other diverse beasts and fowls also that be not seen amongst us.

And the sea is so high that it seemeth as though it hung at the clouds, and that it would cover all the world. And that is great marvel that it might be so, save only the will of God, that the air sustaineth it.

We come to the island called Dondun where there was an idol which, when a person fell sick, decreed whether he should live or die. If the idol decreed death he was suffocated and his family and friends were invited to feast on the body. Anyone who did not attend this ritual was considered to have acted in a highly unneighbourly manner.

But the island of Dondun was surrounded by other islands; and of these and their inhabitants Mandeville's account must be given in full.

Inhabitants of the Islands round Dondun

The king of this isle is a full great lord and a mighty, and hath under him fifty-four great isles that give tribute to him. And in each of these isles is a king crowned; and all be obeissant to that king. And he hath in those isles many diverse folk.

In one of these isles be folk of great stature, as giants. And they be hideous for to look upon. And they have but one eye, and that is in the middle of the front. And they eat nothing but raw flesh and raw fish.

And in another isle toward the south dwell folk of foul stature and of cursed kind that have no heads. And their eyes be in their shoulders.

And in another isle be folk that have the face all flat, all plain, without nose and without mouth. But they have two small holes, all round, instead of their eyes, and their mouth is flat also without lips.

And in another isle be folk of foul fashion and shape that have the lip above the mouth, so great that when they sleep in the sun they cover all the face with that lip.

And in another isle there be little folk, as dwarfs. And they be two so much [twice as large] as the pigmies. And they have no mouth; but instead of their mouth they have a little round hole, and when they shall eat or drink, they take through a pipe or a pen [quill] or such a thing, and suck it in, for they have no tongue, and therefore they speak not, but they make a manner of hissing as an adder doth, and they make signs one to another as monks do, by the which every of them understandeth other.

And in another isle be folk that have great ears and long, that hang down to their knees.

And in another isle be folk that have horses' feet. And they be strong and mighty, and swift runners; for they take wild beasts with running, and eat them.

And in another isle be folk that go upon their hands and their feet as beasts. And they be all skinned and feathered, and they will leap as lightly into trees, and from tree to tree, as it were squirrels or apes.

And in another isle be folk that be both man and woman, and they have kind [nature] of that one and of that other. And they have but one pap on the one side, and on the other none. And they have members of generation of man and woman, and they use both when they list, once that one and another time that other. And they get children when they use the member of man; and they bear children when they use the member of woman.

And in another isle be folk that go always upon their knees full marvellously. And at every pace that they go it seemeth that they would fall. And they have in every foot eight toes.

Many diverse folk of diverse natures be there in other isles about, of the which it were too long to tell, and therefore I pass over shortly.

This gallery of freaks and monsters, which delighted poets no less than simple people, was among the things that later destroyed Mandeville's reputation as a traveller. Instead of letting it be inferred that he had seen them all himself he might have played safe, as he does on other occasions, and confessed that he was only repeating what he had read in the work of Vincent of Beauvais (see Appendix B) and possibly examined in the *Mappa Mundi*. But after all, it did not greatly matter, since his reputation outlived him by several hundred years.

We are still in Ind, but now the Indies are left behind. The country that Mandeville calls Mancy comprised roughly the provinces of Kwang-si and Kwang-tung in southern China.

The Kingdom of Mancy

From these isles, in passing by the sea ocean toward the east by many days' journey, men find a great country and a great kingdom that men call Mancy. And that is in Ind the more. And it is the best land and among the fairest that may be in all the world, and the most delectable and the most plenteous of all goods that is in power of man. In that land dwell many Christian men and Saracens, for it is a good country and a great. And there be therein more than 2000 great cities and rich, without [not counting] other great towns. And there is more plenty of people there than in any other part of Ind, for the bounty of the country. In that country is no needy man, nor none that goeth on begging. And they be full fair folk, but they be all pale. And the men have thin beards and few hairs, but they be long; but scarcely hath any man passing fifty hairs in his beard, and one hair sits here, another there, as the beard of a leopard or of a cat. In that land be many fairer women than in any other country beyond the sea, and therefore men call that land Albany, because that the folk be white.

And the chief city of that country is called Latorin [Canton], and it is a day's journey from the sea, and it is much greater than Paris. In that city is a great river bearing ships that go to all the coasts in the sea . . . Many good cities there be in that country and men have great plenty and great cheap of all wines and victuals. And there be many churches of religious men, and of their law [religion], and in those churches be idols as great as giants . . . Also in that country be white hens without feathers, but they bear white wool as sheep do here.

The Great Chan with three of his wives and his sons

Cassay: the city of bridges

And from that city after many days' journey is another city, one of the greatest of the world, that men call Cassay [Hanchow], that is to say, the 'City of heaven'. That city is well a fifty mile about, and there be twelve principal gates; and before every gate, a three mile or a four mile in length, is a great town or a great city. That city sits upon a great lake on the sea as doth Venice. And in that city be more than 12,000 bridges. And upon every bridge be strong towers and good, in the which dwell the wardens for to keep the city from the great Chan. And on that one part of the city runneth a great river all along the city. And there dwell Christian men and many merchants and other folk of diverse nations, because that the land is so good and so plenteous . . .

The first report of the city of Hanchow, with its '12,000 bridges', was brought back in 1269 by the father and uncle of Marco Polo (and flatly disbelieved by the Venetians).

The Garden of Beasts

From that city men go by water till they come to an abbey of monks that is fast by, that be good religious men after their faith and law. In that abbey is a great garden and a fair, where be many trees of diverse manner of fruits. And in this garden is a little hill full of delectable trees. In that hill and in that garden be many diverse beasts, as of apes, marmosets, baboons and others. And every day, when the convent of this abbey hath eaten, the almoner let bear the food to the garden, and he smiteth on the garden gate with a clicket [key] of silver that he holdeth in his hand; and anon all the beasts of the hill and of diverse places of the garden come out a 3000 or a 4000; and they come in guise of poor men, and men give them the food in fair vessels of silver, clean over-gilt. And when they have eaten the monk smiteth eftsoons on the garden gate with the clicket, and then anon all the beasts return again to their places that they come from. And they say that these beasts be souls of worthy men that resemble in likeness of those beasts that be fair, and therefore they give them meat for the love of God; and the other beasts that be foul, they say be souls of poor men and of common people. And thus they believe, and no man may put them out of this opinion.

Here there is a point worth noting. The silver 'clicket', or latch-key may be a mistranslation (possibly due to a copyist's error) of the French 'clochette', meaning a little bell. Certainly it sounds more probable that the monk should have summoned the animals with a bell than by banging on the gate with a key. A few pages earlier we have the word 'degrees' used for steps or stair-treads; the French for these is '*degrés*'. And in the account of the pigmies which follows, the word 'malice' is used when plainly it does not mean 'ill-will'; it comes from the French '*malin*', meaning clever or cunning. This use of French words, and there are many others, is one of the reasons for supposing that the book was originally written in French.

The story is now approaching the Land of the Great Chan. After crossing a river called Dalay (the Yangtze Kiang) 'that is the greatest river of fresh water that is in the world', we come to the first of the countries under the Chan's rule.

The Land of Pigmies

That river goeth through the land of Pigmies, where that the folk be of little stature, that be but three span long [about two feet high], and they be right fair and gentle, after their quantities, both the men and the women. And they marry them when they be half year of age and get children. And they live but six year or seven at the most; and he that liveth eight year, men hold him there right passing old. These men be the best workers of gold, silver, cotton, silk and all such things of any that be in the world. And they have oftentimes war with the birds of the country that they take and eat. This little folk neither labour in lands nor in vines; but they have men amongst them of our stature that till the land and labour amongst the vines for them. And of those men of our stature have they as great scorn and wonder as we would have among us of giants, if they were amongst us. There is a good city, amongst others, where there is dwelling great plenty of those little folk, and it is a great city and a fair. And the men be tall that dwell amongst them, but when they get any children they be as little as the pigmies; for the nature of the land is such. The great Chan let keep this city full well, for it is his. And albeit, that the pigmies be little, yet they be full reasonable after their age, and con both wit and good and malice [possess intelligence, moral sense and skill].

From that city go men by the country by many cities and many towns unto a city that men call Jamchay; and it is a noble city and a rich and of great profit. The king of that country is full mighty, and yet he is under the great Chan. And the great Chan hath under him twelve such provinces.

Proceeding northward from Ind, into what are now northern China and Mongolia, we enter the Land of Cathay.

Chapter 6

THE LAND OF CATHAY

The magnificence of the Great Chan – The History of how he got his Name – The Immensity of his Wealth and Power

CATHAY is a great country and a fair, noble and rich, and full of merchants. And ye shall understand, that merchants that come from Genoa or from Venice or from Roumania or other parts of Lombardy, they go by sea and by land eleven months or twelve, or more sometime, ere they may come to the isle of Cathay that is the principal region of all parts beyond; and it is of the great Chan.

Mandeville, as we have seen, was obsessed with the idea of islands. His belief that there was an 'Isle of Cathay', dominating the whole vast region bearing that name, may have arisen from the fact that Nicolo and Maffeo Polo, the father and uncle of Marco, travelled a part of the way by water, crossing the Black Sea and stopping for a time at Sudak, in the Crimea, where a few representatives of Venetian merchant houses were already installed.

Beyond this point lay Russia and the measureless unknown of Mongolia and China – an area of mystery embraced by the word 'Cathay', derived from the name of a Mongol tribe settled in northern China. The word came to be invested with a particular magic, a mingling of fantasy and true report which persisted through the centuries until, like other ancient legends, it became increasingly unreal and even tedious, so that Tennyson could write, in *Locksley Hall*, 'Better fifty of Europe than a cycle of Cathay'. But that poem was a prophetic expression of the Victorian belief in 'progress', the humanist materialism of a world to which China was still virtually a closed book. China, to the Victorians, if it was the country of silk and tea was also the country of the opium trade and the 'treaty ports': an enormous uncharted area of backward, semi-barbarous 'natives' (generally unfriendly) who might be patronised and commercially exploited, but who could not seriously be credited with a civilisation not only far older but in many respects more accomplished than that of the west.

Yet the legend, or the dream, lived on in European minds as it had been evoked by Coleridge at the end of the previous century.

> In Xanadu did Kubla Khan
> A stately pleasure-dome decree:

> Where Alph, the sacred river, ran
> Through caverns measureless to man
> Down to a sunless sea.

This Kubla or Kublai Khan (the name has many variants) was the enlightened despot who in the latter half of the thirteenth century received the father and uncle of Marco Polo with great courtesy at his court, eventually sending them back to Italy with the request that they would return with 'a hundred men learned in the Christian religion, well versed in the seven arts, and able to demonstrate the superiority of their own beliefs' – a mission which they were unable to perform. He was the grandson of Genghis Khan, the master of a huge empire and incomparably (although no European would have admitted it) the greatest and most powerful ruler on earth at that time. Although Kublai died in 1294 – that is to say, some seventy years before Mandeville wrote his book – he is the reality behind Mandeville's 'great Chan'.

The story now takes us 'by many journeys' (in this case a matter of months rather than days of travel) to the ancient city which Mandeville calls Caydon, the capital of Cathay.

The Great Chan

In this city is the siege [seat or residence] of the great Chan in a full great palace and the most passing fair in all the world, of the which the walls be in circuit more than two mile. And within the walls it is all full of other palaces. And in the garden of the great palace there is a great hill, upon the which there is another palace; and it is the most fair and the most rich that any man may devise. And all about the palace and the hill be many trees bearing many diverse fruits. And all about that hill be ditches great and deep, and beside them be great vivaries. And in these vivaries be so many wild geese and ganders and wild ducks and swans and herons that it is without number. And all about these ditches and vivaries is the great garden full of wild beasts. So that when the great Chan will have any disport to take any of the wild beasts or of the fowls, he will let chase them and take them at the windows without going out of his chamber.

This palace, where his siege is, is both great and passing fair. And within the palace, in the hall, there be twenty-four pillars of fine gold. And all the walls be covered within of red skins of beasts that men call panthers, that be fair beasts and well smelling; so that for the sweet odour of those skins no evil air may enter into the palace. Those skins be as red as blood, and they shine so bright against the sun that scarcely may a man behold them. And many folk worship those beasts, when they meet them first at morning, for their great virtue and for the good smell that they have. And those skins they prize more than though they were plate of fine gold.

And in the midst of this palace is the mountour [a bowl or drinking-fountain] for the great Chan, that is all wrought of gold and of precious stones and great pearls. And at four corners of the mountour be four serpents of gold. And all about there are large nets of silk and gold and great pearls hanging all about the mountour. And under the mountour be conduits of beverage that they drink in the emperor's court. And beside the conduits be many vessels of gold, by the which they that be of the household drink at the conduit.

And the hall of the palace is full nobly arrayed, and full marvellously attired on all parts in all things that men apparel with [use to decorate] any hall. And first, at the head of the hall is the emperor's throne, full high, where he sitteth at meat. And that is of fine precious stones and great pearls. And the steps that he goeth up to the table be of precious stones mingled with gold.

And at the left side of the emperor's throne is the throne of his first wife, one degree lower than the emperor; and it is of jasper, bordered with gold and precious stones. And the throne of his second wife is also lower than his first wife; and it is also of jasper bordered with gold. And the throne of the third wife is also more low, by a step, than the second wife. For he hath always three wives with him where that ever he be.

And after his wives, on the same side, sit the ladies of his lineage yet lower, after that they be of estate [according to rank]. And all those that be married have a counterfeit made like a man's foot upon their heads, a cubit long, all wrought with great pearls, fine and orient, and above made with peacocks' feathers and of other shining feathers; and that stands upon their heads like a crest, in token that they be under man's foot and under subjection of man. And they that be unmarried have none such.

And after at the right side of the emperor first sitteth his eldest son that shall reign after him. And he sitteth also one degree lower than the emperor, as do the empresses. And after him sit other great lords of his lineage, every of them a degree lower than the other, as they be of estate.

And the emperor hath his table alone by himself, and every one of his wives hath also her table by herself. And his eldest son and the other lords also, and the ladies, and all that sit with the emperor have tables alone by themselves, full rich. And there is no table but that it is worth an huge treasure of goods.

And under the emperor's table sit four clerks that write all that the emperor saith, be it good, be it evil; for all that he saith must be holden, for he may not change his word nor revoke it.

And at great solemn feasts before the emperor's table men bring great tables of gold, and thereon be peacocks of gold and many other manner of diverse fowls, all of gold and richly wrought and enamelled. And men make them dance and sing, clapping their wings together, and make great noise. And whether it be by craft or by necromancy I know not; but it is a good sight to behold, and a fair; and it is great marvel how it may be. But I have the less marvel, because that they be the most subtle men in all sciences and in all crafts that be in the world; for of subtlety and of malice [skill] and of far-casting [prediction] they pass all men under heaven. And therefore they say themselves that they see with two eyes and the Christian men see but with one, because that they be more subtle than they.

And before the emperor's table stand great lords and rich barons and others that serve the emperor at meat. And no man is so bold to speak a word but if the emperor speak to him; except it be minstrels that sing songs and tell jests or other disports, to solace with the emperor. And before the hall door stand many barons and knights clean armed to keep that no man enter except it be the will or the commandment of the emperor, or but if they be servants or minstrels of the household.

And ye shall understand that my fellows and I, with our yeomen, we served this emperor and were his soldiers fifteen months against the King of Mancy, that held war against him. And the reason was that we had great desire to see his noblesse and the estate of his court and all his governance, to know if it were such as we heard say that it was. And truly we found it more noble and more excellent, and richer and more marvellous, than ever we heard speak of, insomuch that we would never have believed it had we not seen it . . . And albeit that some men will not trow me, but hold it for fable to tell them the noblesse of his person and of his estate and of his court and of the great multitude of folk that he holds, natheles I shall say you a part of him and of his folk, after that I have seen the manner and the ordinance full many a time. And whoso that will may believe me if he will, and whoso will not, may leave also.

First I shall say you why he was called the Great Chan.

Clearly Mandeville had doubts as to how much of this brilliantly coloured picture would be believed; so he brazens it out by saying 'I was there', and the reader can take it or leave it. His account of how the Emperor of Cathay acquired the name of the Great Chan may be summarised.

The story begins with Shem, Cham and Japhet (Mandeville's names for them), the sons of Noah who inherited the earth. The villain of the three was Cham, but he was also the greatest and the most mighty and so 'for his cruelty he took the greater and the best part, toward the east, that is called Asia'. One of his grandsons was 'Nimrod the giant, that was the first king that ever was in the world; and he began the foundation of the tower of Babylon [Babel].'

The descendants of Cham divided into seven nations of which 'the most noble and the most prized' were the Tartars. Among the Tartars was 'an old worthy man that was not rich' named Changuys. One night Changuys was visited in a dream by a knight on a white horse, 'armed all in white', who had been sent by God to tell him that he was to be emperor over all the nations of Cathay. He addressed him as Chan, and it was as Chan that the old man became emperor. But although the nations accepted him at the bidding of the White Knight, the new emperor did not trust them. His method of testing their loyalty was drastic, to say the least. Summoning their leaders he commanded, first, that they should surrender all their possessions to him and thereafter hold only what he chose to give them; and secondly that they should bring their eldest sons and behead them in his presence. All of which they did.

Here a passage must be quoted.

The Story of the Owl

And when the Chan saw that they made none obstacle to perform his commandment, then he thought well that he might trust in them, and he commanded them anon to make them ready and sue [follow] his banner. And after this Chan put in subjection all the lands about him.

Afterward it befell upon a day, that the Chan rode with a few meinie [a small force] for to behold the strength of the country that he had won. And so befell, that a great multitude of his enemies met with him. And for to give good example of hardiness to his people, he was the first that fought, and in the midst of his enemies encountered, and there he was cast from his horse, and his horse slain. And when his folk saw him at the earth, they were all abashed, and thought him dead, and fled every one, and their enemies after and chased them, but they knew not that the emperor was there. And when the enemies were far pursuing the chase, the emperor hid him in a thick wood. And when they [the enemies] were come again from the chase, they went and sought the woods if any of them [the emperor's men] had been hid in the thick of the woods; and many they found and slew them anon. So it happened that as they went searching toward the place that the emperor was, they saw an owl sitting upon a tree above him; and then they said amongst them that there was no man [there] because that they saw that bird there, and so they went their way; and thus escaped the emperor from death. And then he went privily by night, till he came to his folk that were full glad of his coming, and made great thankings to God Immortal, and to that bird by whom their lord was saved. And therefore principally above all fowls of the world they worship the owl. And when they have any of their feathers they keep them full preciously instead of relics, and bear them upon their heads with great reverence; and they hold themselves blessed and safe from all perils while they have them upon them, and therefore they bear their feathers upon their heads.

So this first Chan became the ruler of all Asia and founder of a long line of Chans, among them Cobyla Chan (another variant of Kublai) who reigned (says Mandeville) for forty-two years and founded 'the great city of Izonge in Cathay, that is a great deal more than Rome'. This was the Xanadu of Coleridge's poem, the modern city of Shandu. Mandeville tells us, for no reason, that Cobyla was a Christian, but adds that his successors reverted to paganism. He goes on to describe the four ceremonial feasts held each year by the Chan, one being to celebrate his birthday. These great ceremonies were conducted by four thousand 'barons, mighty and rich', divided into companies of a thousand, those in the first company being of the highest rank. Each company was clad in silk robes of its own colour – green, red, blue and yellow, in order of precedence – but all were of unparalleled splendour.

And all their clothes be so nobly and so richly wrought with gold and precious stones and rich pearls, that if a man of this country had but only one of their robes he might well say that he should never be poor; for the gold and the precious stones and the great orient pearls be of greater value on this half the sea [the west] than they be beyond the sea in those countries.

And when they be thus apparelled they go two and two together full ordinately before the emperor, without speech of any word, save only inclining to him. And every one of them beareth a tablet of jasper or of ivory or of crystal, and the minstrels going before them, sounding their instruments of diverse melody. And when the first thousand is passed and hath made its muster, it withdraweth to one side; and then entereth the second thousand, and doth the same; and after, the third; and then, the fourth; and none of them saith not one word.

And at one side of the emperor's table sit many philosophers that be proved for wise men in many diverse sciences, as of astronomy, necromancy, geomancy, pyromancy, hydromancy, of augury and of many other sciences. And all have before them instruments of gold, some spheres, some the brain pan of a dead man, some vessels of gold full of gravel or sand, some vessels of gold full of water and of wine and of oil, and some horologes [timepieces] of gold, made full nobly and richly wrought, and many other manner of instruments after their sciences.

And at certain hours, when them thinketh time, they say to certain officers that stand before them, ordained for the time to fulfil their commandments: Make peace!

And then say the officers: Now peace! Listen.

And after that, saith another of the philosophers: Every man do reverence and incline to the emperor, that is God's Son and sovereign lord of all the world! For now is time! And then every man boweth his head toward the earth.

And then commandeth the same philosopher again: Stand up! And they do so.

And at another hour, saith another philosopher: Put your little finger in your ears! And anon they do so.

And at another hour, saith another philosopher: Put your hand before your mouth! And anon they do so.

And at another hour, saith another philosopher: Put your hand upon your head! And after that he biddeth them to do their hand away. And they do so.

Which is not far removed from the three monkeys with eyes, ears and mouth covered – 'See no evil, hear no evil, speak no evil' – evil, in this case, being against the Chan, and the hand on the head a gesture of allegiance. After this feudal ritual there followed a procession of great nobles bringing gifts. Then the minstrels played, and then it was the turn of the magicians, masters of hallucination. This is a famous passage.

The Magicians

And then come jugglers and enchanters, that do many marvels; for they make to come in the air, by seeming, the sun and the moon to every man's sight. And after they make the night so dark that no man may see nothing. And after they make the day to come again, fair and pleasant with bright sun. And then they bring in dances of the fairest damsels of the world, and richest arrayed. And after they make to come in other damsels bringing cups of gold full of milk of diverse beasts, and give drink to lords and to ladies. And then they make knights to joust in arms full lustily; and they run together a great random, and they frussch [clash] together full fiercely, and they break their spears so rudely that the truncheons fly in sprouts and pieces all about the hall. And then they make to come in hunting for the hart and for the boar, with hounds running with open mouth. And many other things they do by craft of their enchantments, that it is marvel for to see. And such plays of disport they make till the taking up of the boards.

The number of the Chan's servants and retainers was so great that Mandeville measures them in 'cumants' – a cumant being ten thousand men. There were thirteen cumants of minstrels (mercifully, not all were present at court at the same time) and fifteen cumants of yeomen to look after the Chan's collection of birds and beasts, ranging from ostriches and popinjays [parrots] to elephants and every kind of monkey. There were also four hundred and ten Christian doctors and leeches.

The Chan could afford to be a lavish spender because he manufactured his own money. He did not waste gold and silver, using the precious metals solely for ornament, but printed his currency on leather or paper – 'and when that money hath run so long that it beginneth to waste, then men bear it to the emperor's treasury and they take new money for the old'.

The Chan's formal 'progresses' through his realm were decidedly impressive.

And when this emperor will ride from one country to another he or-daineth four hosts of his folk, of the which the first host goeth before him a day's journey. For that host shall be lodged the night where the emperor shall lie upon the morrow. And in this first host is the number of people fifty cumants, of horse and of foot, of the which every cumant amounteth 10,000, as I have told you before. And another host goeth on the right side of the emperor, nigh half a day's march from him. And another goeth on the left side of him, in the same wise. And in every host is as much multitude of people as in the first host. And then after cometh the fourth host, that is much more than any of the others, and that goeth behind him, the distance of a bow draught [a bowshot]. And every host hath his journeys ordained in certain places, where they shall be lodged at night, and there they shall have all that them needeth . . .

And ye shall understand that the empire of this great Chan is divided in twelve provinces; and every province hath more than two thousand cities, and of towns without number. This country is full great, for it hath twelve principal kings in twelve provinces, and every of those kings have many kings under them, and all they be obeissant to the great Chan. And his land and his lordship dureth [extends] so far, that a man may not go from one head to another, neither by sea nor land, the space of seven year. And through the deserts of his lordship, there as men may find no towns, there be inns ordained by every journey to receive both man and horse, in the which they shall find plenty of victual, and of all things that they need for to go by the country.

One hundred and thirty thousand minstrels (but the word may also have meant craftsmen), one hundred and fifty thousand game wardens and an escorting army of well over two million soldiers who would have stripped the countryside bare if the Chan had in fact employed so many on his progresses! All this is Mandeville's superb embellishment of the more modest facts supplied him by Marco Polo and the Franciscan monk, Odoric. He may well have had misgivings, wondering if even the most credulous reader would swallow it. He is on safer ground when he describes the high-speed messenger service which the Chan must certainly have needed.

And there is a marvellous custom in that country (but it is profitable), that if any contrarious thing [happen] that should be prejudice or grievance to the emperor in any kind, anon the emperor hath tidings thereof and full knowledge in a day, though it be three or four journeys from him or more. For his ambassadors take their dromedaries or their horses, and they prick in all that ever they may [go at full gallop] towards one of the inns. And when they come there, anon they blow an horn. And anon they of the inn know well enough that there be tidings to warn the emperor of some rebellion against him. And then anon they make other men ready in all haste that they may to bear letters, and prick in all that ever they may till they come to the other inns with their letters. And then they make fresh men ready, to prick forth with the letters toward the emperor, while that the last bringer rest him, and bait his dromedary or his horse. And so, from inn to inn, till it come to the emperor. And thus anon hath he hasty tidings of anything that beareth charge, by his couriers, that run so hastily throughout all the country. And also when the Emperor sendeth his couriers hastily throughout his land, every one of them hath a large thong full of small bells, and when they draw near to the inns of other couriers that be also ordained by the journeys, they ring their bells, and anon the other couriers make them ready, and run their way unto another inn. And thus runneth one to other, full speedily and swiftly, till the emperor's intent be served in all haste.

The account of local customs in the next chapter is also recognisably based on true report. We may end this chapter with Mandeville's own summing up.

Under the firmament is not so great a lord, nor so mighty, nor so rich as is the great Chan; not Prester John, that is emperor of the high Ind, nor the Soldan of Babylon, nor the Emperor of Persia. All these be not in comparison to the great Chan, neither of might, nor of noblesse, nor of royalty, nor of riches; for in all these he passeth all earthly princes. Wherefore it is great harm that he believeth not faithfully in God. And natheles he will gladly hear speak of God. And he suffereth well that Christian men dwell in his lordship, and that men of his faith be made Christian men if they will, throughout all his country; for he defendeth [forbids] no man to hold no law [faith] other than him liketh.

The Great Chan hiding in a thick wood with the owl sitting on a tree
above him

The Great Chan in progress

Chapter 7

CATHAY AND BEYOND

The People of Tartary – The Land of Darkness – Beyond Cathay – The Country of the Jews – The Griffins

THE 'Tartarians dwelling in Cathay', about whom Mandeville now writes, were the Mongols. This huge conglomerate of nomadic tribes from central Asia, under such remarkably able leaders as Genghis Khan and Kublai Khan, had in the twelfth and thirteenth centuries established an enormous, if insecure, empire embracing virtually the whole of China, extending through Russia to eastern Europe, engulfing the Holy Land for a time and even penetrating into India, where they founded the Mogul dynasty. Tales of the Mongols' warlike ability, their savagery and ruthlessness, particularly under Genghis, had filtered through to the west, making of them a subject of awe and terrified speculation. Were they to be regarded as an even greater potential threat to Christendom than the more immediate threat of Islam? Or on the other hand, since whatever else they were they were not Moslems, might they be made into an ally, a counter-balance to Islam?

These questions were, in fact, in process of being answered while Mandeville was engaged in writing his book. After Kublai Khan the Mongol hold on China steadily weakened. It might have been restored by the great Tamerlane (Timur the Lame) but he died before he could carry out his plans. The Mongol empire crumbled. In 1368 the dynasty of Mongol Khans in China was overthrown and replaced by the Chinese Ming dynasty, an event which changed the world. Under the Ming emperors and their successors China reverted to its age-old state of isolation. The Mongol thirst for foreign conquest, and the Mongol tolerance of foreign peoples and creeds, both were abandoned. For a period of four or five centuries, behind frontiers closed to all 'barbarians' (in particular those from the west), the great Chinese empire, indifferent to the rest of the world, pursued its own life, enacted its own often sanguinary dramas, developed its own art and philosophy in its own way.

But that lay in the future. For the present, for Mandeville's readers, to whom Cathay was a word of mystery, enchantment and possible peril, there was a particular interest in what he now relates.

Of the Law and the Customs of the Tartarians dwelling in Cathay

The folk of that country use all long clothes without furs. And in the same manner as the men go, the women go, so that a man may scarcely know the men from the women, save only those women that be married, that bear the token upon their heads of a man's foot. And their wives dwell not together, but each of them by herself. Each hath his house, both man and woman. And their houses be made round of staves, and have a round window above that giveth them light and also that serveth for deliverance of smoke. And when they go to war, they lead their houses with them upon chariots, as men do tents or pavilions. And they make their fire in the midst of their houses.

They begin all their things in the new moon, and they worship much the moon and the sun and often-time kneel to them. And all the folk of the country ride commonly without spurs, but they bear always a little whip in their hands for to chase with their horses.

They be all good archers and shoot right well, both men and women, as well on horse-back, pricking, as on foot, running. And the women make all things and all manner of mysteries and crafts, as of clothes, boots and other things; and they drive carts, ploughs and wains and chariots; and all the women wear breeches, as well as men.

All the folk of that country be full obeissant to their sovereigns; they fight not, nor chide one with another. And there be neither thieves nor robbers in that country. And every man worshippeth other; but no man there doth reverence to strangers, but if they be great princes.

And they eat hounds, lions, leopards, mares and foals, asses, rats and mice and all manner of beasts great and small, save only swine and beasts that were defended by the old law. And they eat but little bread, but if it be in courts of great lords. And the rich men drink milk of mares or of camels or of asses or of other beasts. And they will be lightly drunken of milk and of another drink that is made of honey and of water sodden together; for in that country is neither wine nor ale. They eat but once in the day, and that but little, neither in courts nor in other places. And in sooth, one man alone in our country will eat more in a day than one of them will eat in three days. And if any strange messenger come there to a lord, men make him to eat but once a day, and that full little.

And when they war, they war full wisely and always do their business, to destroy their enemies. All their lust and all their imagination is for to put all lands under their subjection. And they say that they know well by their prophecies, that they shall be overcome by archers and by strength of them;

66

but they know not of what nation nor of what law they shall be of, that shall overcome them. And therefore they suffer that folk of all laws [religions] may peaceably dwell amongst them.

And when any man shall die, men set a spear beside him. And when he draweth towards the death, every man fleeth out of the house till he be dead. And after that they bury him in the fields.

And when the emperor dieth, men set him in a chair in midst the place of his tent. And men set a table before him clean, covered with a cloth, and thereupon flesh and diverse viands and a cup full of mare's milk. And men put a mare beside him with her foal, and an horse saddled and bridled. And they lay upon the horse gold and silver, great quantity. And they put about him great plenty of straw. And then men make a great pit and a large, and with the tent and all these other things they put him in earth. And they say that when he shall come into another world, he shall not be without an house, nor without horse, nor without gold and silver; and the mare shall give him milk, and bring him forth more horses till he be well stored in the tother world. For they trow that after their death they shall be eating and drinking in that other world, and solacing them with their wives, as they did here . . .

And then, after the death of the emperor, the seven lineages assemble them together and choose his eldest son, or the next after him of his blood. And thus they say to him; we will and we pray and ordain that ye be our lord and our emperor.

And then he answereth, If ye will that I reign over you as lord, do each of you that I shall command him, either to abide or to go; and whomsoever that I command to be slain, anon he shall be slain.

And they answer all with one voice, Whatsoever ye command, it shall be done.

Then saith the emperor, Now understand well, that my word from henceforth is sharp and biting as a sword.

In all this there was a good deal of truth, although it is strange that Mandeville, talking of 'a drink that is made of honey and water sodden together', should not have mentioned mead. He now leaves Cathay, which was in 'Asia the deep', and moves on into 'Asia the more'. We hear in passing of many kingdoms – Tharsia, Turkestan, Khorasan – all of which paid allegiance to the Great Chan; and then Comania, which was the old name for Hungary but which in Mandeville's account seems to have embraced most of Russia. The story at this point has become a travelogue, its geography bewildering.

Now, since I have devised you the lands and the kingdoms toward the parts Septentrionals in coming down from the land of Cathay into the lands of the Christian, towards Prussia and Russia – now shall I devise you of other lands and kingdoms coming down by other coasts, toward the right side, unto the sea of Greece, toward the land of Christian men. And, therefore, that after Ind and after Cathay the Emperor of Persia is the greatest lord, therefore I shall tell you of the kingdom of Persia.

But in fact Mandeville has little to say about Persia, and nothing of particular interest. We pass on to Armenia, Media and the kingdom of Georgia, which, we are told, was divided into two kingdoms, both ruled by Christian kings. One of these was the kingdom of Abchaz.

The Land of Darkness

In that kingdom of Abchaz is a great marvel. For a province of the country that men call Hanyson is all covered with darkness, without any brightness or light; so that no man may see or hear, nor no man dare enter into it. And, natheles, they of the country say that sometimes men hear voice of folk, and horses neighing, and cocks crowing. And men wit well that men dwell there, but they know not what men. And they say that the darkness befell by miracle of God. For a cursed emperor of Persia, named Saures, pursued all Christian men to destroy them and to compel them to make sacrifice to his idols, and rode with great host for to confound the Christian men. And then in that country dwelled many good Christian men, the which left their goods and would have fled into Greece. And when they were in a plain called Megon, anon this cursed emperor met with them with his host for to have slain them and hewn them to pieces. And anon the Christian men kneeled to the ground and made their prayers to God to succour them. And anon a great thick cloud came and covered the emperor and all his host. And so they endure in that manner that they may not go out on no side; and so shall they evermore abide in that darkness till the day of doom, by the miracle of God. And then the Christian men went where them liked best, at their own pleasance, without letting [hindrance] of any creature, and their enemies enclosed and confounded in darkness, without any stroke.

All this seems to have been somewhere in the region of the Caucasus. We proceed to Turkey, Mesopotamia, Mauretania, Ethiopia and Libya, glancing briefly at each.

And after is Lybia the high and Lybia the low, that descendeth down low toward the great sea of Spain, in the which country be many kingdoms and many diverse folk.

Now I have devised you many countries on this half the kingdom of Cathay, of the which many be obeissant to the great Chan.

At which point the story finally moves beyond the 'lordship' of Cathay.

The Miraculous Fruit

In passing by the land of Cathay toward the high Ind and toward Bacharia [Bactria], men pass by a kingdom that men called Caldilhe [possibly Korea], that is a full fair country.

And there groweth a manner of fruit, as though it were gourds. And when they be ripe, men cut them a-two, and men find within a little beast, in flesh, in bone and blood, as though it were a little lamb without wool. And men eat both the fruit and the beast. And that is a great marvel. Of that fruit I have eaten, although it were wonderful [scarcely to be believed], but that I know well that God is marvellous in his works. And, natheles, I told them of as great a marvel to them, that is amongst us, and that was of the Bernakes [barnacle geese]. I told them that in our country were trees that bear a fruit that become birds flying, and those that fall in the water live, and they that fall on the earth die anon, and they be right good to man's meat. And hereof had they as great marvel, that some of them trowed it were an impossible thing to be.

Barnacle geese – birds hatched out of the fruit of a tree – were a part of English folklore that persisted long after Mandeville's time. John Gerard in his *Herball or General Historie of Plantes*, published in 1597, gives an account of them at second-hand, but which, he says, 'may very well accord with truth'. The two stories that follow call for no comment. They are tales that were told.

The Country of the Jews

In that same region be the mountains of Caspian that men call Uber in the country. Between those mountains the Jews of ten lineages [tribes] be enclosed, that men call Goth and Magoth, and they may not go out on no side. There were enclosed twenty-two kings with their people, that dwelled between the mountains of Scythia. There King Alexander chased them between those mountains, and there he thought for to enclose them through work of his men. But when he saw that he might not do it, nor bring it to an end, he prayed to God of nature that he would perform that which he had begun. And although that he was a paynim and not worthy to be heard, yet God of his grace closed the mountains together, so that they dwell there all fast locked and enclosed with high mountains all about, save only on one side, and on that side is the sea of Caspian.

Now may some men ask, since that the sea is on that one side, wherefore go they not out on the sea side, for to go where that them liketh?

But to this question, I shall answer; that sea of Caspian goeth out by land under the mountains, and runneth by the desert at one side of the country, and after it stretched unto the ends of Persia, and although it be called a sea it is no sea, nor it toucheth to none other sea, but it is a lake, the greatest of the world; and were they to put them into that sea they know not where they should arrive; and also they can no language but only their own, that no man knoweth but they; and therefore may they not go out.

And also ye shall understand that the Jews have no proper land of their own for to dwell in, in all the world, but only that land between the mountains. And yet they yield tribute for that land to the Queen of Amazonia, the which that maketh them to be kept in close full diligently, that they shall not go out on no side but by the coast of their land; for their land marcheth to those mountains.

The Griffins

From that land go men toward the land of Bacharia where be full evil folk and full cruel. In that land be trees that bear wool, as though it were of sheep, whereof men make clothes and all things that may be made of wool.

In that country be many hippotaynes [hippopotamus] that dwell sometime in the water and sometime on the land. And they be half man and half horse, as I have said before. And they eat men when they may take them.

And there be rivers of waters that be full bitter, three times more than is the water of the sea.

In that country be many griffins, more plenty than in any other country. Some men say that they have the body upward as an eagle and beneath as a lion; and truly they say sooth, that they be of that shape. But one griffin hath the body more great and is more strong than eight lions, of such lions as be on this half, and more great and stronger than an hundred eagles such as we have amongst us. For one griffin there will bear, flying to his nest, a great horse, if he may find him at the point, or two oxen yoked together as they go at the plough. For he hath talons so long and so large and great upon his feet, as though they were horns of great oxen or of bugles [young bulls] or of kine, so that men make cups of them to drink of. And of their ribs and of the pens [pinions] of their wings, men make bows, full strong, to shoot with arrows.

From thence go men by many journeys through the land of Prester John, the great Emperor of Ind. And men call his realm the Isle of Pentexoire.

Chapter 8

THE LAND OF PRESTER JOHN

The Christian Emperor – The Sea of Gravel – The Old Man of the Mountain – The Valley Perilous – Why Prester John was so called

THE LEGEND of a Christian empire situated somewhere in the remote east and ruled by a monarch who called himself John the Priest grew up mysteriously in the twelfth century. Like other legends, it may have had some basis of fact. An isolated Christian community or tribe may have established itself in some place beyond the bounds of Christendom, to be magnified by rumour into a great empire; although later research suggests that, if it existed at all, it was more likely to have been in Abyssinia than anywhere in Asia. But what gave the story substance was the circulation of a letter supposedly written by Prester John to the Emperor Manuel I of Byzantium (1143–1180). This letter, filled with wonders and absurdities, was a fabrication, the work of an unknown author; but at the time, and for long afterwards, many men believed it, including Mandeville.

Mandeville's narrative is here particularly discursive. Although it is derived mainly from the forged letter (which he also draws upon in other parts of his book: for instance, his mention of the Well of Youth) he introduces matter from other sources.

We are told at the start why traders and others were indisposed to visit the land of Prester John.

This emperor, Prester John, holds full great land and hath many noble cities and good towns in his realm, and many great diverse isles and large. For all the country of Ind is devised in isles for the great floods that come from Paradise, that divide all the land in many parts. And also in the sea he hath full many isles. And the best city in the Isle of Pentexoire is Nyse, that is a full royal city and a noble, and full rich.

This Prester John hath under him many kings and many isles and many diverse folk of diverse conditions. And this land is full good and rich, but not so rich as is the land of the great Chan. For the merchants come not thither so commonly for to buy merchandises, as they do in the land of the great Chan, for it is too far to travel to. And on that other part, in the Isle of Cathay, men find all manner thing that is need to man, cloths of gold, of silk, of spicery and all manner avoirdupois [merchandise]. And therefore, albeit that men have greater cheap in the Isle of Prester John, natheles, men dread the long way and the great perils in the sea in those parts.

For in many places of the sea be great rocks of stones of the adamant, that of his proper nature draweth iron to him. And therefore there pass no ships that have either bonds or nails of iron within them. And if there do, anon the rocks of the adamants draw them to them, that never they may go thence. I myself have seen afar in that sea, as though it had been a great isle full of trees and buscaylle [undergrowth], full of thorns and briars, great plenty. And the shipmen told us, that all that was of ships that were drawn thither by the adamants, for the iron that was in them.

The Prester John letter, although it was a compound of invention, rumour and travellers' report, was not without elements of truth. A concentration of magnetic rock (adamant) could certainly divert a ship from its course by causing a deviation in its (lodestone) compass; on the other hand, it seems unlikely that the attraction would have been so great as to drag a wooden vessel on to the rocks merely because its timbers were fastened with metal. But the isle full of trees, which were the masts of sunken ships, is a wonderfully vivid picture.

Mandeville now begins to tell of Prester John; but after a page or so he digresses into the story of the Gravelly Sea before returning to the subject. We have altered the sequence so as to keep his account of Prester John, or the bulk of it, in one piece. It has been suggested that the Gravelly Sea may have had some sort of counterpart in the Gobi desert; clearly a very slight one.

The Gravelly Sea

For in his country [Prester John's] is the sea that men call the Gravelly Sea, that is all gravel and sand, without any drop of water, and it ebbeth and floweth in great waves as other seas do, and it is never in peace, in no season. And no man may pass that sea by navy, nor by no manner of craft, and therefore may no man know what land is beyond that sea. And albeit that it have no water, yet men find therein and on the banks full good fish of other manner of kind and shape than men find in any other sea, and they be of right good taste and delicious to man's meat.

And three days' journey from that sea be great mountains out of the which goeth out a great flood that cometh out of Paradise. And it is full of precious stones, without any drop of water, and it runneth through the desert on that one side, so that it maketh the sea gravelly; and it beareth into that sea and there it endeth. And that river runneth but three days in the week and bringeth with him great stones and the rocks also therewith, and that great plenty. And anon, as they be entered into the Gravelly Sea, they be seen no more but lost for evermore. And in those three days that that river runneth, no man dare enter into it; but in the other days men dare enter well enough.

Also beyond that river, more upward to the deserts, is a great plain all gravelly, between the mountains. And in that plain, every day at the sunrising, begin to grow small trees, and they grow till mid-day, bearing fruit; but no man dare take of that fruit, for it is a thing of faerie. And after mid-day they decrease and enter again into the earth, so that at the going down of the sun they appear no more. And so they do every day. And that is a great marvel.

In that desert be many wild men that be hideous to look on; for they be horned and they speak nought, but they grunt as pigs. And there is also great plenty of wild hounds. And there be many popinjays, that they call psittakes in their language. And they speak of their proper nature, and salute men that go through the deserts, and speak to them as apertly [clearly] as though it were a man.

Prester John

This Emperor Prester John taketh always to his wife the daughter of the great Chan; and the great Chan also, in the same wise, the daughter of Prester John. For these two be the greatest lords under the firmament.

In the land of Prester John be many diverse things and many precious stones, so great and so large that men make of them vessels, as platters, dishes and cups. And many other marvels be there, that it were too cumbrous and too long to put it in scripture of books; but of the principal isles and of his estate and of his law, I shall tell you some part.

This Emperor Prester John is Christian, and a great part of his country also. But yet they have not all the articles of our faith as we have. They believe well in the Father, in the Son and in the Holy Ghost. And they be full devout and right true one to another. And they set no store by barretts nor by cautels [fraud and trickery], nor of no deceits. And he hath under him seventy-two provinces, and in every province is a king. And these kings have kings under them, and all be tributaries to Prester John.

And when he goeth into battle against any other lord, he hath no banners borne before him; but he hath three crosses of gold, fine, great and high, full of precious stones, and each of those crosses be set in a chariot, full richly arrayed. And for to keep guard every cross be ordained 10,000 men of arms and more than 100,000 men on foot, in manner as men would keep a standard in our countries, when that we be in land of war. And this number of folk is without [additional to] the principal host and without wings ordained for the battle. And when he hath no war, but rideth with a privy meinie [escort], then he hath borne before him but one cross of tree [wood], without painting and without gold or silver or precious stones, in remembrance that Jesu Christ suffered death upon a cross of tree. And he hath borne before him also a platter of gold full of earth, in token that his noblesse and his might and his flesh shall turn to earth; and also a vessel of silver, full of noble jewels of gold full rich and of precious stones, in token of his lordship and of his noblesse and of his might.

He dwelleth commonly in the city of Susa. And there is his principal palace, that is so rich and so noble that no man will trow it by estimation [imagine it], but he had seen it. And above the chief tower of the palace be two round pommels of gold, and in each of them be two carbuncles [globes] great and large, that shine full bright upon the night. And all the pillars in his chamber be of fine gold with precious stones, and with many carbuncles, that give great light upon the night to all people. And albeit that the carbuncles give light right enough, natheles at all times burneth a vessel of crystal full of balm, for to give good smell and odour to the emperor, and to void away all wicked airs and corruptions. And the form of his bed is of fine sapphires, bended with gold, for to make him sleep well and to refrain him from lechery; for he will not lie with his wives except four times in the year, after the four seasons, and that is only for to engender children.

He hath also a full fair palace and a noble at the city of Nyse, where that he dwelleth, when him best liketh; but the air is not so attempre [mild], as it is at the city of Susa.

This Emperor Prester John hath evermore seven kings with him to serve him, and they depart [divide] their service by certain months. And with these kings serve always seventy-two dukes and three hundred and sixty earls. And all the days of the year, there eat in his household and in his court twelve archbishops and twenty bishops. And the patriarch of Saint Thomas is there as is the Pope here. And the archbishops and the bishops and the abbots in that country be all kings. And the land dureth in very breadth four months' journeys, and length out of measure, that is to say, all the isles under earth that we suppose to be under us.

What follows is founded on fact. The religious sect of the Assassins, of which the leader became known as the Old Man of the Mountain, was established in the mountains of Persia in 1090, and for nearly two centuries terrorised the Moslem world by the murder of statesmen, generals and high officials. Its trained killers were drugged with hashish, from which the word 'assassin' is derived. This macabre oriental mingling of religious fanaticism and politics is a strange enough episode, even without Mandeville's adornments.

The Old Man of the Mountain

Beside the isle of Pentexoire, that is the land of Prester John, is a great isle, long and broad, that men call Mistorak; and it is in the lordship of Prester John. In that isle is great plenty of goods.

There was dwelling, sometime, a rich man; and it is not long since; and men called him Gatholomabes. And he was full of cunning and subtle deceits. And he had a full fair castle in a mountain, so strong and so noble that no man could devise a fairer or stronger. And he had let mure [enclosed] all the mountain about with a strong wall and a fair. And within those walls he had the fairest garden that any man might behold. And therein were trees bearing all manner of fruits, and many fair wells; and beside those wells he had let make fair halls and fair chambers, painted all with gold and azure; and there were in that place many diverse things, and many diverse stories [contrivances]: of beasts and birds that sung full delectably and moved by craft, that it seemed that they were quick [alive]; and he had also in his garden all manner of fowls and of beasts that any man might think on, for to have play or sport to behold them.

And he had also in that place the fairest damsels that might be found, under the age of fifteen years, and the fairest young striplings that men might get, of that same age. And all they were clothed in cloths of gold, full richly. And he said that those were angels. And that place he called Paradise.

And when that any good knight, that was hardy and noble, came to see this royalty, he would lead him into his paradise, and show him these wonderful things to his disport, and the marvellous and delicious song of diverse birds, and the fair damsels, and the fair wells of milk, of wine and of honey, plenteously running. And he would let make divers instruments of music to sound in an high tower, so merrily, that it was joy for to hear; and no man should see the craft thereof [how it was done]. And those, he said, were angels of God. And then would he make them to drink of certain drink, whereof anon they should be drunk. And then would they think greater delight than they had before. And then would he say to them, that if they would die for him and for his love, after their death they should come to his paradise; and after that yet should he put them in a fairer paradise, where that they should see God of nature visibly, in his majesty and in his bliss. And then would he shew them his intent, and say them, that if they would go slay such a lord, or such a man that was his enemy, that they should not dread to do it

Griffins

The well in Paradise showing the beginning of the Rivers Ganges, Nile,
Tigris and Euphrates

and for to be slain therefore themselves. For after their death, he would put them into another paradise, that was an hundred-fold fairer than any of the tother; and there should they dwell with the most fairest damosels that might be, and play with them evermore.

And thus went many diverse lusty bachelors for to slay great lords in diverse countries, that were his enemies, and made themselves to be slain, in hope to have that paradise. And thus, oftentime, he was revenged of his enemies by his subtle deceits and false cautels [stratagems].

And when the worthy men of the country had perceived the subtle falsehood of this Gatholomabes, they assembled them with force and assailed his castle and slew him, and destroyed all the fair places and all the nobilities of that paradise. The place of the wells and of the walls and of many other things be yet clearly seen, but the riches is voided clean. And it is not long gone since that place was destroyed.

The Assassins were in fact rooted out of their mountain fastness by the Mongols in 1256, about a hundred years before Mandeville wrote his account of them.

We are still in 'the lordship of Prester John'. The story that follows is one which had so great an impact that echoes of it are constantly to be found in seventeenth- and eighteenth-century literature – for example, in Bunyan's 'Valley of the Shadow of Death'. Mandeville, who got it from Friar Odoric (Appendix B), so embellished it that, whatever basis of fact it may have had, he has made it into fantasy. Its dark and terrible nature may perhaps explain why he felt that he could only convince his readers by assuring them that he was there.

The Valley Perilous

Beside that Isle of Mistorak upon the left side nigh to the river of Pison is a marvellous thing. There is a vale between the mountains that dureth nigh a four mile. And some men call it the Vale Enchanted, some call it the Vale of Devils, and some call it the Vale Perilous. In that vale hear men often-time great tempests and thunders, and great murmurs and noises, all days and nights, and great noise, as it were sound of tabors and of nakers [drums] and of trumps, as though it were of a great feast. This vale is all full of devils, and hath been always. And men say there that it is one of the entries of hell. In that vale is great plenty of gold and silver. Wherefore many misbelieving men, and many Christian men also, go in oftentime for to have of the treasure that there is; but few return, namely of the misbelieving men nor of the Christian men neither, for anon they be strangled of devils.

And in mid place of that vale, under a rock, is an head and the visage of a devil bodily, full horrible and dreadful to see, and it sheweth not but the head, to the shoulders. But there is no man in the world so hardy, Christian man or other, but that he would be adread to behold it, and that it would seem him to die for dread, so is it hideous for to behold. For he beholdeth every man so sharply with dreadful eyen that be evermore moving and sparkling as fire, and changeth and stirreth so often in diverse manner, with so horrible countenance, that no man dare draw near him. And from him cometh out smoke and stinking fire and so much abomination, that scarcely may a man there endure.

But the good Christian men, that be stable in the faith, enter well without peril. For they will first shrive them and mark them with the token of the holy cross, so that the fiends have no power over them. But albeit that they be without peril, yet natheles be they not without dread when that they see the devils visibly and bodily all about them, that make full many diverse assaults and menaces, in air and in earth, and aghast them with strokes of thunder-blasts and of tempests. And the most dread is, that God will take vengeance then of that that men have misdone against his will.

And ye shall understand that when my fellows and I were in that vale we were in great thought, whether that we durst put our bodies in adventure, to go in or not, in the protection of God. And some of our fellows accorded to enter, and some not. So there were with us two worthy men, friars minors [Franciscans], that were of Lombardy, that said that if any man would enter they would go in with us. And when they had said so, upon the gracious trust of God and of them, we let sing mass, and made every man to be shriven and houselled [receive communion]. And then we entered fourteen persons; but at our going out we were but nine. And we knew never whether that our fellows were lost, or else turned back for dread. But we saw them never after; and those were two men of Greece and three of Spain. And our other fellows that would not go in with us, they went by another coast to be before us; and so they were.

And thus we passed that perilous vale, and found therein gold and silver and precious stones and rich jewels, great plenty, both here and there, as us seemed. But whether that it was, as us seemed, I wot never. For I touched none, because that the devils be so subtle to make a thing to seem otherwise than it is, for to deceive mankind. And therefore I touched none, and also because that I would not be put out of my devotion; for I was more devout then than ever I was before or after, and all for the dread of fiends that I saw in diverse figures, and also for the great multitude of dead bodies that I saw there lying by the way, by all the vale, as though there had been a battle between two kings, and the mightiest of the country, and that the greater part had been discomfited and slain. And I trow that scarcely should any country have so much people within it as lay slain in that vale as us thought, the which was an hideous sight to see. And I marvelled much that there were so many, and the bodies all whole without rotting. But I trow that fiends made them seem so to be whole without rotting. And many of them were in habit of Christian men, but I trow well that it were of such that went in for covetise of the treasure that was there, and had overmuch feebleness in the faith; so that their hearts might not endure in the belief for dread. And therefore were we the more devout a great deal. And yet we were cast down, and beaten down many times to the hard earth by winds and thunders and tempests. But evermore God of his grace help us. And so we passed that perilous vale without peril and without encumbrance, thanked be Almighty God.

This concludes the story of the Valley Perilous; but Mandeville goes straight on to tell of other marvels, mainly derived from the Letter.

After this, beyond the vale, is a great isle, where the folk be great giants of twenty-eight foot long, or of thirty foot long. And they have no clothing but of skins of beasts that they hang upon them. And they eat no bread, but all raw flesh; and they drink milk of beasts, for they have plenty of all bestial. And they have no houses to lie in. And they eat more gladly man's flesh than any other flesh. Into that isle dare no man gladly enter. And if they see a ship and men therein, anon they enter into the sea for to take them.

And men said us, that in an isle beyond that were giants of greater stature, some of forty-five foot, or of fifty foot long, and, as some men say, some of fifty cubits long. But I saw none of those, for I had no lust to go to those parts, because that no man cometh neither into that isle nor into the other but that he be devoured anon. And among those giants be sheep as great as oxen here, and they bear great wool and rough. Of the sheep I have seen many times. And men have seen, many times, those giants take men in the sea out of their ships, and bring them to land, two in one hand and two in another, eating them as they go, all raw and alive.

Another isle is there toward the north, in the sea Ocean, where that be full cruel and full evil women of nature. And they have precious stones in their eyen. And they be of that kind, that if they behold any man with wrath, they slay him anon with the beholding, as doth the basilisk.

There were yet other islands, inhabited by people who were at least human, strange though their customs sometimes were. But the wild life was often even stranger. The 'camles' which are here described – about the size of a goat – can only have been chameleons.

There also be many beasts, that be called orafles [giraffes]. In Arabia they be called gerfaunts. That is a beast, dappled or spotted, that is but a little more high than is a steed, but he hath the neck a twenty cubits long; and his croup and his tail are as of an hart, and he may look over a great high house. And there be also in that country many camles; that is a little beast as a goat, that is wild, and he liveth by the air and eateth nought, nor drinketh nought, at no time. And he changeth his colour often-time, for men see him often, now in one colour and now in another colour; and he may change him into all manner of colours that him list, save only into red and white. And there be lions all white, great and mighty. And there be also other beasts, as great and more greater than is a destrier [charger], and men call them loerancs; and they have a black head and three long horns in the front, sharp as a sword, and the body is slender; and this is a full felonious beast, and he chaseth and slayeth the elephant. And there be also mice as great as hounds, and yellow mice as great as ravens. And many other diverse beasts be in those countries, and elsewhere there-about, and many diverse birds also, of the which it were too long for to tell you. And therefore, I pass over at this time.

The chapter ends with a last word on Prester John.

Many other isles there be in the land of Prester John, and many great marvels, that were too long to tell all, both of his riches and of his noblesse and of the great plenty also of precious stones that he hath. I trow that ye know well enough, and have heard say, wherefore this emperor is called Prester John. But, natheles, for them that know not, I shall say you the cause.

It was sometime an emperor there, that was a worthy and a full noble prince, that had Christian knights in his company, as he hath that is now. So it befell, that he had great list [desire] for to see the service in the church among Christian men. And then dured Christendom beyond the sea, all Turkey, Syria, Tartary, Jerusalem, Palestine, Arabia, Aleppo and all the land of Egypt. And so it befell that this emperor came with a Christian knight with him into a church in Egypt. And it was the Saturday in Whitsun week. And the bishop made orders. And he beheld and listened the service full tentively. And he asked the Christian knight what men of degree they should be that the prelate had before him. And the knight answered and said that they should be priests. And then the emperor said that he would no longer be called king nor emperor, but priest, and that he would have the name of the first priest that went out of the church, and his name was John. And so ever since, he is called Prester John.

Chapter 9

THE END OF THE JOURNEY

The Hills of Gold guarded by Ants – The Garden of Eden – The Rich Man – Farewell

MANDEVILLE still has a few marvels up his sleeve. The story of the hills of gold guarded by ants, whatever we may think of it as natural history, is notable as an allegory.

The Hills of Gold

Toward the east part of Prester John's land is an isle good and great that men call Taprobane, that is full noble and full fructuous. In that isle be great hills of gold, that pismires [ants] keep full diligently. And they fine the pured gold, and cast away the un-pured. And these pismires be great as hounds, so that no man dare come to those hills, for the pismires would assail him and devour him anon. So that no man may get of that gold, but by great sleight [cunning]. For when it is great heat the pismires rest them in the earth, from prime of the day into noon. And then the folk of the country take camels, dromedaries and horses and other beasts and go thither, and load them in all haste that they may; and after that they flee away in all haste that the beasts may go, ere the pismires come out of the earth. And in other times, when it is not so hot, and that the pismires rest them not in the earth, then they get gold by this subtlety. They take mares that have young colts or foals, and lay upon the mares void vessels made there-for; and they be all open above, and hanging low to the earth. And then they send forth those mares for to pasture about those hills, and keep the foals with them at home. And when the pismires see those vessels, they leap in anon: and they have this kind nature that they let nothing be empty among them but anon they fill it, be it whatever manner of thing; and so they fill those vessels with gold. And when that the folk suppose that the vessels be full, they put forth anon the young foals and make them to neigh after their dams. And then anon the mares return towards their foals with their charges of gold. And then men discharge them, and get gold enough by this subtlety. For the pismires will suffer beasts to go and pasture amongst them, but no man in no wise.

We come now to a matter which is at the heart of Mandeville's book and indeed of most ancient thinking. Mandeville's geography was based on immemorial beliefs that had been somewhat modified by the birth of Christ, which caused Christian men to regard (or adopt) Jerusalem as the centre of the world. The *Mappa Mundi* gives us a picture of that world as a whole, but Mandeville is here concerned only with the Paradise Terrestrial, that is to say, the Garden of Eden, from which flowed the four great rivers which were believed to be the source of all fresh water upon earth. The names he uses are variants of those given in the Book of Genesis, except in the case of the third, the Tigris, which Genesis calls Hiddekel.

The Garden of Eden

And beyond the land and the isles and the deserts of Prester John's lordship, in going straight toward the east, men find nothing but mountains and rocks, full great. And there is the dark region, where no man may see, neither by day nor by night, as they of the country say. And that desert and that place of darkness dure from this coast unto Paradise Terrestrial, where that Adam, our foremost father, and Eve were put, that dwelled there but little while: and that is towards the east at the beginning of the earth.

Of Paradise can I not speak properly. For I was not there. It is far beyond. And also I was not worthy. But as I have heard say of wise men beyond, I shall tell you with good will.

Paradise Terrestrial, as wise men say, is the highest place of earth, that is in all the world. And it is so high that it toucheth nigh to the circle of the moon, there as the moon maketh her turn; for she is so high that the flood of Noah might not come to her, that would have covered all the earth of the world all about and above and beneath, save Paradise only alone. And this Paradise is enclosed all about with a wall, and men know not whereof it is made; for the walls be covered all over with moss, as it seemeth. And it seemeth not that the wall is stone of nature, nor made of any other thing that is known. And that wall stretcheth from the south to the north, and it hath not but one entry that is closed with fire, burning; so that no man that is mortal dare enter.

And in the most high place of Paradise, even in the middle place, is a well that casteth out the four floods that run by divers lands. Of the which, the first is called Pison, or Ganges; and it runneth throughout Ind or Emlak, in the which river be many precious stones, and much of lignum aloes and much gravel of gold. And that other river is called Nilus or Gison, that goeth by Ethiopia and after by Egypt. And that other is called Tigris, that runneth by Assyria and by Armenia the great. And that other is called Euphrates, that runneth also by Media and Armenia and by Persia. And men there beyond say that all the sweet waters of the world, above and beneath, take their beginning of the well of Paradise, and out of that well all waters come and go.

And ye shall understand that no man that is mortal may not approach to that Paradise. For by land no man may go for wild beasts that be in the deserts, and for the high mountains and great huge rocks that no man may pass by, for the dark places that be there, and that many. And by the rivers may no man go. For the water runneth so rudely and so sharply, because that it cometh down so outrageously from the high places above, that it runneth in so great waves, that no ship may not row nor sail against it. Many great lords have assayed with great will many times for to pass by those rivers towards Paradise, with full great companies. But they might not speed in their voyage. And many died for weariness of rowing against those strong waves. And many of them became blind, and many deaf, for the noise of the water. And some were perished and lost within the waves. So that no mortal man may approach to that place, without special grace of God, so that of that place I can say you no more; and therefore I shall hold me still, and return to that, that I have seen.

The journey is very near its end. There is a last, charming story to be told (with a highly moral sting in its tail) which is recognisably derived from Mandeville's reading about China, although he situates it as usual on 'another good isle' ten days' journey from the land of the great Chan.

The Rich Man

And in that country is a passing rich man, that is no prince nor duke nor earl, but he hath more that hold of him lands and other lordships, for he is more rich. For he hath every year of annual rent 300,000 horses charged with corn of diverse grains and of rice. And so he leadeth a full noble life and a delicate, after the custom of the country. For he hath, every day, fifty fair damosels, all maidens, that serve him evermore at his seat, and for to lie by him o' night, and for to do with them that is to his pleasance. And when he is at table they bring him his meat at every time, five and five together; and in bringing their service they sing a song. And after that they cut his meat and put it in his mouth; for he toucheth nothing, nor handleth nought, but holdeth ever more his hands before him upon the table. For he hath so long nails, that he may take nothing, nor handle nothing. For the noblesse of that country is to have long nails, and to make them grow always to be as long as men may. And the noblesse of the women is for to have small feet and little. And therefore anon as they be born, they let bind their feet so strait that they may not grow half as nature would. And always these damosels, that I spake of before, sing all the time that this rich man eateth. And when that he eateth no more of his first course, then other five and five fair damsels bring him his second course, always singing as they did before. And so they do continually every day to the end of his meat. And in this manner he leadeth his life. And so did those before him, that were his ancestors. And so shall they that come after him without doing of any deeds of arms, but live evermore thus in ease, as a swine that is fed in sty for to be made fat.

And then it is over. Mandeville (we are told) returned to Rome, where he submitted his book to the Pope 'that it might be examined and corrected by advice of his wise and discreet council.'

And our holy father, of his special grace, remitted my book to be examined and proved by the advice of his said council. By the which my book was proved for true, insomuch that they shewed me a book that my book was examined by [compared with], that comprehended full much more, by an hundred part, by the which the *Mappa Mundi* was made after. And so my book (albeit that many men list not to give credence to nothing but to that that they see with their eye, be the author never so true) is affirmed and proved by our holy father, in manner and form as I have said.

The sad fact about that challenging assertion is that the Pope was not then in Rome During the period from 1309 to 1377 (roughly Mandeville's own lifetime) the seat of the Papacy was Avignon, where a succession of popes occupied the bleak, grandiose pile of the Palais des Papes, which today echoes with the footsteps of tourists. But we may not blame Mandeville for the error. The passage does not appear in the French or Latin versions of his book, but only in the English version. It would be interesting to know why the English translator inserted it. Did he have private doubts about Mandeville's veracity, and feel that the book needed this reinforcement? Or on the other hand, believing in it implicitly, did he want to compel the reader to do the same?

And what would Mandeville himself have thought? As we know, he was not over-scrupulous in these matters. Probably he would have acquiesced, if he thought he could get away with it.

But is it really important? That the book is built on an imposture may be deplored, but there is much more to be said on the credit side. Nowhere do we find in it any trace of coarseness of mind, no dwelling on horror for horror's sake, nothing at all that today might be classed as pornography; this shortened version has needed no 'editing' in that sense. It is a pleasant book, inspired by love and reverence for life, staunchly Christian but tolerant of other creeds, always more ready to marvel and admire than to condemn; a book by a decent and lovable man for whom James Elroy Flecker's lines might well have been written:

What shall we tell you? Tales, marvellous tales
  Of ships and stars and isles where good men rest,
Where nevermore the rose of sunset pales
  And winds and shadows fall toward the West.

That is what Mandeville was: a storyteller, nothing more. As he takes sad leave of us, an ageing man tormented by arthritic gout (in spite of having drunk from the Well of Youth!) we may surely return his salute.

And I, John Mandeville, knight, abovesaid (although I be unworthy), that departed from our countries and passed the sea, the year of grace 1322, that have passed many lands and many isles and countries, and searched many full strange places, and have been in many a full good honourable company, and at many a fair deed of arms, (albeit that I did none myself, for mine unable insuffisance), now that I am come home, maugre myself, to rest, for gouts artetykes that me distrain that define the end of my labour; against my will (God knoweth).

And thus, taking solace in my wretched rest, recording the time past, I have fulfilled these things, and put them written in this book, as would come into my mind, the year of grace 1356, in the thirty-fourth year that I departed from our countries. Wherefore I pray to all the readers and hearers of this book, if it please them, that they will pray to God for me and I shall pray for them.

Amen! Amen! Amen!

THE END

Appendix A

THE EARTH IS ROUND

The idea that the earth was a sphere, not flat, was far from new in Mandeville's time. Egyptian, and later Greek, astronomers had propounded it a thousand years before the birth of Christ, although they also believed that the sun went round the earth. But Christian orthodoxy in Mandeville's day still maintained that the earth was a circular disc ringed round by ocean and suspended immovably in space, held there by God's hand, with Jerusalem at its centre, the sun and stars (the firmament) revolving round it, and Heaven and Hell somewhere beyond. It was not until the sixteenth century that Copernicus upset this apple-cart by demonstrating that the earth moved round the sun, while also revolving on its own axis. His work seems to have had little immediate impact outside scientific circles; but when, in the next century, Galileo published a book endorsing the theory, he got into serious trouble with the Church.

Mandeville, in the fourteenth century, did not doubt that the sun went round the earth; but he was no less sure that the earth was a sphere, inhabited all over. The fact that he felt compelled to argue the case, and did so with such care, is an indication of how far he was challenging the conventional wisdom.

He had evidently given much thought to the matter. Whether, as he tells us, he had gone so far as to master the use of the astrolabe may be questioned. It was a difficult contrivance, a crude but elaborate device for taking altitudes and establishing latitude, used in astronomy and navigation, and in some sort a forerunner of the modern sextant. But certainly he had pored over the works of the astronomers, whose misapprehensions he generally shared. For example, the belief in a fixed star in the south (the Antarctic Star) corresponding to that other fixed star, the Star Transmontane, or North Star, was a common one, and few travellers from the west had been far enough south of the equator, or often enough or long enough, to disprove it.

Science could not be divorced from religious faith – indeed, it perhaps never can be. In an age when the law of gravity had still to be propounded the great stumbling-block to the round-earth theory was the inexplicable fact that men on earth's underneath side, so to speak, did not fall off, and seemed to themselves to be walking the right way up when they were walking upside-down. Mandeville meets this with a simple reference to the Creator – 'Do not fear [mistrust] Me, who have suspended earth in the void.' It was an unanswerable position, and still is.

He cites in evidence stories of men who have circumnavigated the earth and come back to the place where they started; he makes elaborate calculations designed to establish the earth's circumference (and in fact is not so very far out); and at the end, with his mention of 'climates', he seems to be touching on the field of astrology, so closely related to the matter in hand. We need not discuss any of this in detail. The passage is not a contribution to present scientific knowledge, nor is it an essential part of Mandeville's book. It is interesting and important in two respects, as a noteworthy example of the scientific argument of the time and for the light it throws on Mandeville himself. So we have detached it from the main body of the book and placed it here, separate and intact, with a few textual elucidations but no gloss, for the benefit of those readers who may be disposed to study it. The less scientifically-minded will probably prefer to let it go.

The Argument

In that land [the Isle of Lamary] and in many other beyond that, no man may see the Star Transmontane [the North Star] that is called the Star of the Sea, that is unmovable and that is toward the north, that we call the Lode-star. But men see another star, the contrary to him, that is toward the south, that is called Antarctic. And right as the ship-men take their advice here and govern them by the Lode-star, right so do ship-men beyond those parts by the star of the south, the which star appeareth not to us. And this star that is toward the north, that we call the Lode-star, appeareth not to them. For which cause men may well perceive that the land and the sea be of round shape and form; for the part of the firmament sheweth in one country that sheweth not in another country. And men may well prove by experience and subtle compassment of wit, that if a man found passages by ships that would go to search the world, men might go by ship all about the world and above and beneath.

The which thing I prove thus after that I have seen. For I have been toward the parts of Brabant, and beholden [by means of] the Astrolabe that the star that is called the Transmontane is fifty-three degrees high; and more further in Almayne [Germany] and Bohemia it hath fifty-eight degrees; and more further toward the parts septentrional [northern] it is sixty-two degrees of height and certain minutes; for I myself have measured it by the Astrolabe. Now shall ye know, that against the Transmontane is the tother star that is called Antarctic, as I have said before. And those two stars move never, and by them turneth all the firmament right as doth a wheel that turneth by his axle-tree. So that those stars bear the firmament in two equal parts, so that it hath as much above it as it hath beneath. After this, I have gone toward the parts meridional, that is, toward the south, and I have found that in Lybia men see first the star Antarctic. And so far I have gone more further in those countries that I have found that star more high; so that toward the High

Lybia it is eighteen degrees of height and certain minutes (of the which sixty minutes make a degree). After going by sea and by land toward this country of which I have spoken, and to other isles and lands beyond that country, I have found the Star Antarctic of thirty-three degrees of height and more minutes. And if I had had company and shipping for to go more beyond, I trow well, in certain, that we should have seen all the roundness of the firmament all about. For, as I have said to you before, the half of the firmament is between those two stars, and which halvendel [half] I have seen. And of the tother halvendel I have seen, toward the north under the Transmontane, sixty-two degrees and ten minutes, and toward the part meridional I have seen under the Antarctic, thirty-three degrees and sixteen minutes. And then, the halvendel of the firmament in all holdeth but nine score degrees. And of those nine score, I have seen sixty-two on that one part and thirty-three on the other part; that be, ninety-five degrees and nigh the halvendel of a degree. And so, there it is that I have seen all the firmament, save four score and four degrees and the halvendel of a degree, and that is not the fourth part of the firmament; for the fourth part of the roundness of the firmament holds four score and ten degrees, so there faileth but five degrees and an half of the fourth part. And also I have seen the three parts of all the roundness of the firmament and more yet five degrees and a half. By the which I say you certainly that men may environ [go round] all the earth of all the world, as well under as above, and return again to their country, that have company and shipping and conduct [navigation], and always he should find men, lands and isles, as well as in this country. For ye wit well, that they that be toward the Antarctic, they be straight, feet against feet, of them that dwell under the Transmontane; also well as we and they that dwell under us be feet against feet. For all the parts of sea and of land have their opposites, habitable or trespassable, both they of this half and the beyond half.

And wit well, after that that I may perceive and comprehend, that the lands of Prester John, Emperor of Ind, be under us. For in going from Scotland or from England toward Jerusalem men go upward always. For our land is in the low part of the earth toward the west, and the land of Prester John is in the low part of the earth toward the east. And they have there the day when we have the night; and also, high to the contrary, have they the night when we have the day. For the earth and the sea be of round form and shape, as I have said before; and that that men go upward to one coast, men go downward to another coast.

Also ye have heard me say that Jerusalem is in the midst of the world. And that may men prove, and shew there by a spear that is pight [thrust] into the earth upon the hour of mid-day, when it is equinox, that sheweth no shadow on no side. And that it should be in the midst of the world, David witnesseth it in the Psalter, where he saith, *Deus operatus est salutem in medio terrae* [God hath worked salvation in the midst of the earth]. Then they that depart from those parts of the west for to go toward Jerusalem, as many journeys may they go from Jerusalem unto other confines of the superficiality of the earth beyond. And when men go beyond those journeys toward Ind and to the foreign isles, all is environing the roundness of the earth and of the sea under our countries on this half.

And therefore hath it befallen many times of one thing that I have heard counted when I was young, how a worthy man departed sometime from our countries for to go search the world. And so he passed Ind and the isles beyond Ind, where be more than 5000 isles. And so long he went by sea and land, and so environed the world by many seasons, that he found an isle where he heard speak his own language, calling on oxen in the plough, such words as men speak to beasts in his own country; whereof he had great marvel, for he knew not how it might be. But I say, that he had gone so long by land and by sea that he had environed all the earth; that he was come again environing, that is to say, going about, unto his own marches, and if he had gone further he had found his country and his own knowledge. But he turned back. And so he lost much painful labour, as himself said a great while after that he was come home. For it befell later that he went into Norway. And there tempest of the sea took him, and he arrived in an isle. And, when he was in that isle, he knew well that it was the isle where he had heard speak his own language before and the calling of oxen at the plough; and that was possible thing.

But how it seemeth to simple men unlearned, that men may not go under the earth, and also that men should fall toward the heaven from under. But that may not be, upon less than we may fall toward heaven from the earth where we be. For from what part of the earth that men dwell, either above or beneath, it seemeth always to them that dwell that they go more right than any other folk. And right as it seemeth to us that they be under us, right so it seemeth to them that we be under them. For if a man might fall from the earth unto the firmament, by greater reason the earth and the sea that be so great and so heavy should fall to the firmament: but that may not be, and therefore saith our Lord God, *Non timeas me, qui suspendi terram ex nihilo.* [Do not mistrust me, who have suspended earth in the void.]

And albeit that it be possible thing that men may so environ all the world, natheles, of a thousand persons, one might not happen to return into his country. For, for the greatness of the earth and of the sea, men may go by a thousand and a thousand other ways, that no men could ready [steer] him perfectly toward the parts that he came from, but if it were by adventure and hap [chance], or by the grace of God. For the earth is full large and full great, and holds in roundness and about environ, by above and by beneath, 20,425 miles, after the opinion of old wise astronomers; and their sayings I reprove nought. But, after my little wit, it seemeth me, saving their reverence, that it is more.

And for to have better understanding I say thus. Be there imagined a figure that hath a great compass. And, about the point of the great compass that is called the centre, be made another little compass. Then after, be the great compass devised by lines in many parts, and that all the lines meet at the centre. So, that in as many parts as the great compass shall be departed [divided], in as many shall be departed the little, that is about the centre, albeit that the spaces be less. Now then, be the great compass represented for the firmament, and the little compass represented for the earth. Now then, the firmament is devised by astronomers in twelve signs, and every sign is devised in thirty degrees. That is, 360 degrees that the firmament hath above. Also, be the earth devised in as many parts as the firmament, and let every part answer to a degree of the firmament. And wit it well, that, after the authors of astronomy, 700 furlongs of earth answer to a degree of the firmament, and those be eighty-seven miles and four furlongs. Now be that here multiplied by 360 sithes [times], and then they be 31,500 miles every of eight furlongs, after miles of our country. So much hath the earth in roundness and of height environ, after mine opinion and mine understanding.

And ye shall understand that after the opinion of old wise philosophers and astronomers, our country nor Ireland nor Wales nor Scotland nor Norway nor the other isles coasting to them be not in the superficiality counted above the earth, as it sheweth by all the books of astronomy. For the superficiality of the earth is parted in seven parts for the seven planets, and those parts be called climates. And our parts be not of the seven climates, for they be descending toward the west drawing towards the roundness of the world. And also these isles of Ind which be even against us be not reckoned in the climates. For they be against us that be in the low country. And the seven climates stretch them environing the world.

Appendix B

MANDEVILLE'S SOURCES

Marco Polo

The Travels of Marco Polo is a book to be read for its own sake and one which needs no introduction here. A few essential facts may be noted. Marco's father and uncle, the Venetian merchants Nicolo and Maffeo Polo, were the first westerners of repute to penetrate to the depths of Cathay. This was in the year 1260, or thereabouts. Being hospitably received at the court of Kublai Khan they returned there some years later, taking with them the youthful Marco, who became a person of some consequence under the Emperor, whom he served for seventeen years. Shortly after his return home, in the year 1298, Marco was captured and imprisoned by the Genoese, with whom Venice was then at war.

It was during his period of imprisonment, which seems to have lasted only for a few months, that his book was written. But he did not write it himself. He told it to a certain Rusticello of Pisa, a fellow-prisoner and a professional writer of romances – and 'what he told', we learn from the prologue, 'was only what little he was able to remember.' Rusticello wrote it down (or up) in his own fashion, adding flourishes, and probably embellishments, of his own.

In short, this most famous of all travel books is a 'ghosted' work, true in substance, we need not doubt, but certainly not always reliable in detail. And although it is Mandeville's best-known source – indeed, the only one which is now remembered – it is not necessarily the most important. It relates only to the latter half of Mandeville's Travels, and its author's alert, observant eye was essentially that of a practical man of affairs, neither a scholar nor an historian. Mandeville drew upon many other sources, and without the help of the next name on this list his book could scarcely have been written.

Vincent of Beauvais

A thirteenth-century scholar of prodigious industry and erudition. His *Speculum majus*, written in Latin and translated into French in about 1330, was one of the earliest encyclopedias, a compilation in four large volumes embracing the whole field of knowledge and quoting some hundreds of authors, ranging from Strabo and Pliny to Carpini, who is mentioned below. The huge work was Mandeville's constant source of reference. Details from it crop up everywhere in his book, notions of geography and natural history and, to quote one specific instance, the array of freaks and monsters inhabiting the islands round Dondun.

John de Plano Carpini

A Franciscan missionary whose account of the Mongol world was the first to reach Christendom. He preceded the Polos. Setting out from Lyon in 1245, he was received by Mangu Khan, the brother and predecessor of Kublai, in 1246, and was home again in 1247 – a feat of rapid travel and endurance which so undermined his health that he died soon after. But not before he had written his book, which was of particular interest for its account of the lives and customs of the Mongol people. Much of Mandeville's information on the subject came from this source, but possibly indirectly, by way of the *Speculum majus*, in which most of it was incorporated.

Odoric of Pordenone

Friar Odoric was of the greatest value to Mandeville. He was another Franciscan missionary, of later date than Carpini or the Polos, having started on his travels in about the year 1316. His was a very roundabout journey. He spent some time in India and the East Indies before eventually reaching Peking. Mandeville's account of Indian religious practices is derived largely from Odoric.

But so is much else in his book, in particular the story of the Valley Perilous. Because of its extraordinary nature, and also for the light it throws on Mandeville's methods as a story-teller, Odoric's account of this episode is worth quoting in full.

'There was another terrible thing which I saw there: for passing by a certain valley, which is situate beside a pleasant river, I saw many dead bodies, and in the said valley also I heard divers sweet sounds and harmonies of music, especially the noise of citherns, whereat I was greatly amazed. This valley containeth in length seven or eight miles at the least, into the which whosoever entereth, dieth presently, and can by no means pass alive through the midst thereof: for which cause all the inhabitants thereabout decline unto the one side. Moreover, I was tempted to go in, and to see what it was. At length making my prayers, and recommending myself to God in the name of Jesu, I entered, and saw such swarms of dead bodies there as no man would believe unless he were an eye-witness thereof. At the one side of the foresaid valley, upon a certain stone, I saw the visage of a man, which beheld me with such a terrible aspect that I thought verily I should have died in the same place. But always this sentence, The Word became flesh and dwelt amongst us, I ceased not to pronounce, signing myself with the sign of the cross, and nearer than seven or eight paces I durst not approach unto the said head: but I departed and fled unto another place in the said valley, ascending up into a little sandy mountain, where looking round about, I saw nothing but the said citherns, which methought I heard miraculously sounding and playing by themselves without the help of musicians. And being upon the top of the mountain, I found silver there like the scales of fishes in great abundance: and I gathered some part thereof into my bosom to show for a wonder, but my conscience rebuking me, I cast it up the earth, reserving no whit at all unto myself, and so, by God's grace, I departed without danger. And when the men of the country knew that I was returned out of the valley alive, they reverenced me much.'

Clearly something happened. Odoric was a prosaic-minded, generally un-imaginative man, but an honest one. When he tells us that he himself entered the valley and was terrified by what he experienced, we may believe him. Some such place must surely have existed, a place so eerie – impregnated, perhaps, with the memory of past disaster – that it induced in him visions or hallucinations of the kind that we now attribute to extra-sensory perception. But consider Mande-ville's version of the same episode (pp. 77–79). It is twice as long. The story is made more circumstantial by the inclusion of a party of companions; and the drama and terror are so heightened as to lift it off the earth into the realm of fantasy. This was at once Mandeville's weakness and his strength, the reason for his popu-larity. Men *wanted* to believe in marvels. A further word may be added. When later the two books, Mandeville's and Odoric's, were compared and found to differ, as they constantly do, it was Mandeville who was believed, not Odoric.

Haiton (or Heyton) the younger

A member of the ruling house of Armenia who died in 1308. His *Fleur des Histoires d'Orient*, a book dealing with the geography of Asia and the history of Egypt and the Tartars, supplied Mandeville with a great deal of material, including the story of how the Great Chan came to be so called.

William of Boldensele

A German who travelled extensively in Egypt and the Holy Land. Probably the most useful of the many writers, some very ancient, upon whom Mandeville drew for the early chapters of his book. He was one of those who believed that the pyramids were tombs, a view which Mandeville rejected, preferring the legend of the Garners of Joseph.

The Letter of Prester John

Some account of this forgery has already been given. All that need be added here is that Marco Polo, too, seems to have been taken in by it.

The full, long list of Mandeville's sources, probable and possible, is a matter for scholars. The short list given here is at least sufficient to refute the charge, so often levelled against Mandeville, that he was nothing but an inventor, or in plain words a liar, another Münchhausen. He was a great embroiderer, a great toucher-up of stories; he exaggerated, sometimes wildly. But he pored over his books, he had a great respect for knowledge; and, in fact, he invented very little.

Appendix C

THE MAPPA MUNDI

Whether Mandeville actually saw the great Hereford *Mappa Mundi*, which was made in about the year 1300 and is still preserved in the cathedral, cannot be certainly known; but its relevance to his book is very evident.

The map is the work of Richard de Haldingham and Lafford, who became a prebendary of Hereford Cathedral in 1305. To call it a map in the sense in which we now use the word is misleading. It is a fanciful depiction of the world as it was supposed to be. It is very large – 63 inches high by 54 inches broad – and crowded with detail, place-symbols, mythical beasts, legendary allusions, with numerous inscriptions in Latin or, occasionally, Norman French. A photographic reproduction capable of being fitted into this volume would be far too small to be of value. We have used a modern artist's drawing, showing the map in outline with only a little of the detail.

It depicts the flat circle of earth ringed round by ocean, with Heaven at the top, beyond the circumference, and the Garden of Eden (or Earthly Paradise) immediately below it, just within the circle. Jerusalem is exactly at the centre. To relate the map to our geography we have to turn it on its side so that Heaven is to the east. The Great Sea, the Mediterranean, is depicted as a huge right-angle, its lower half extending westward from the Holy Land to the Pillars of Hercules, that is to say, Gibraltar. The upright half, extending to Constantinople, has four arms, of which one, the westward arm, approximates to the Adriatic. The middle eastward arm extends roughly into Asia Minor, and the upper eastward arm approximates to the Black Sea and the Caspian. The north-eastern part of the map is broadly Ind and Cathay, the north-western quarter is Europe, and the southern part is, very roughly, Africa and the undefined region that Mandeville called Dondun. There is, of course, no America or Australasia.

But this kind of approximation is not really helpful. It is better to forget geography and see the map for what it is, a piece of pictorial folklore and a depiction of Mandeville's world. Many of its details figure in his narrative, the Dry Tree, the Sciapods, the Phoenix, the Garners of Joseph and others. They are a part of the imaginative inheritance out of which his book was made. It is worth remembering that the map preceded the book by some seventy years.

Appendix D

FURTHER READING

The reader who wishes to embark upon the whole of Mandeville has two excellent complete texts with modern spelling at his disposal. The earlier, and the one used by the compilers of this book (it also includes the writings of Carpini and Odoric) was edited by the late Professor A. W. Pollard and published by Macmillan in 1900. A very much more recent version, which does not however differ substantially from the Pollard text, has been prepared by M. C. Seymour, who has also edited a text in the original spelling with invaluable footnotes. Both these volumes are published by the Oxford University Press.

Two works dealing with the subject as a whole, and to which the compilers of this volume must make grateful acknowledgement, are:

Sir John Mandeville: The Man and His Book by Malcolm Letts (The Batchworth Press, London, 1949);

Mandeville Rediscovered by Josephine Waters Bennett (The Modern Language Association of America, 1954).

The first of these, which is relatively short, is a scholarly and charming work intended for the general reader. The second, which is designed for specialists and students, is very much more exhaustive and in particular examines in detail the numerous manuscript versions in different languages.

As to the books which in one way or another have a bearing on the subject, but deserve, in any case, to be read for their own sake, the list is endless. Three, in particular, may be noted:

The Travels of Marco Polo, of which a new translation by Robert Latham was published by Penguin Books in 1958 and has since been frequently reprinted;

Mediaeval People, by Eileen Power, also published by Penguin;

Travel and Travellers of the Middle Ages, edited by A. P. Newton, published by Routledge & Kegan Paul in 1949.

Garden of Eden

Sciapod

Noah's Ark

Golden Fleece

*Black
Sea*

Jerusalem

Dog People

Constantinople

E U R O P E

British Isles